Transforming Qualitative Information

This book is dedicated to
David C. McClelland

During the past 50 years, you provoked, coaxed, coached, and challenged us, your graduate students and colleagues, into learning how to use thematic analysis to extend our curiosity. Thank you, David. Whatever the value of our insights, discoveries, and their applications, you made it possible!

Transforming Qualitative Information

THEMATIC ANALYSIS AND CODE DEVELOPMENT

RICHARD E. BOYATZIS

SAGE Publications
International Educational and Professional Publisher
Thousand Oaks   London   New Delhi

For information:

SAGE Publications, Inc.
2455 Teller Road
Thousand Oaks, California 91320
E-mail: order@sagepub.com

SAGE Publications Ltd.
6 Bonhill Street
London EC2A 4PU
United Kingdom

SAGE Publications India Pvt. Ltd.
M-32 Market
Greater Kailash I
New Delhi 110 048 India

Printed in the United States of America

Boyatzis, Richard E.
    Transforming qualitative information: Thematic analysis and
code development / by Richard E. Boyatzis.
        p. cm.
    Includes bibliographical references (p.   ) and index.
    ISBN 0-7619-0960-5 (cloth: acid-free paper). — ISBN
0-7619-0961-3 (pbk.: acid-free paper)
    1. Social sciences—Research. 2. Social sciences—Methodology.
3. Qualitative reasoning.   I. Title.
H62.B628   1998
300′.72—dc21   97-45405

This book is printed on acid-free paper.

06   07   08   09   11   10   9   8

Acquisition Editor:	Peter Labella
Editorial Assistant:	Corinne Pierce
Production Editor:	Michele Lingre
Production Assistant:	Denise Santoyo
Typesetter/Designer:	Rose Tylak
Cover Designer:	Ravi Balasuriya
Print Buyer:	Anna Chin

Contents

Preface

Qualitative methods have had a rough time gaining acceptance in the mainstream of social and behavioral science research. One of the major reasons has been the lack of methods for bridging or translating between the worlds of qualitative and quantitative research. In addition, the rich tapestry of information in qualitative sources has often eluded or intimidated researchers. The topic of this book, thematic analysis, is a process that many have used in the past without articulating the specific techniques. It is a process used as part of many qualitative methods. In this sense, it is not a separate method, such as grounded theory or ethnography, but something to be used to assist the researcher in the search for insight.

Scholars and researchers from many fields use thematic analysis. Some examples from different fields are Aesop's *Fables,* in which the moral is the result of a thematic analysis; Freudian or Jungian dream analysis; identification of patterns of enabling behavior in families of alcoholics; ethnographic approaches to analysis of child rearing in various cultures; participant observation studies of street gangs; analysis of shifts in marketplace sentiment and preferences; and analysis of the changing climate in the workforce in organizations.

Thematic analysis is a process for encoding qualitative information. The encoding requires an explicit "code." This may be a list of themes; a complex model with themes, indicators, and qualifications that are causally related; or something in between these two forms. A theme is a pattern found in the information that at the minimum describes and organizes possible observations or at the maximum interprets aspects of the phenomenon. A theme may be identified at the manifest level (directly observable in the information) or at the latent level (underlying the phenomenon). The themes may be initially generated inductively from the raw information or generated deductively from theory and prior research. The compilation or integration of a number of codes in a study is often called a *codebook*.

Although the process has had widespread use, there has been little written to help people learn the technique. It has typically been passed from an experienced professional to a professional in training like the motto of a secret society. In rare cases, a person seems to have an intuitive grasp of the process, probably resulting from his or her specific combination of cognitive complexity, cognitive style, and a few other perceptual, synthetic, and analytic capabilities.

When people from different countries who speak different languages meet for the first time, a translator facilitates communication. Thematic analysis is a translator of those speaking the language of qualitative analysis and those speaking the language of quantitative analysis; it also enables those who use different qualitative methods to communicate with each other. Further, it allows a researcher with a qualitative method and design to translate observations and apply statistical analysis to determine validity of the themes or code if that approach to determining validity is desired. Descriptive use of thematic analysis is desirable if the particular methodology chosen for a study requires enhancing the clarity of results or findings and the ease of communication. In providing access to discoveries and insights generated through qualitative methods, thematic analysis expands the possible audience for the communication and dissemination of ideas and results. Thematic analysis allows researchers using quantitative methods to incorporate operant and open-ended measures or forms of information collection into their designs.

In the books, monographs, and papers on qualitative methods, typically no more than a few pages and occasionally a whole chapter are devoted to the specific techniques that yield a thematic analysis. Some recent exceptions to this observation are Silverman (1993), Wolcott (1994), Coffey and Atkinson (1996), and Mason (1996). Furthermore, professionals tend to learn thematic analysis as it applies to one type of information (e.g., dreams, observed group interaction, market preferences, sexual rites of passage). This inhibits the spread of the method and its use in exploring complex, multidisciplinary phenomena, for which it is probably the only way to begin thoughtful inquiry.

The objective of this book is to teach the process of thematic analysis: that is, to help people learn how to develop thematic codes with which to observe and perceive people, groups, organizations, cultures, or events. This includes helping readers learn how to sense themes. Many researchers already have developed the ability to sense themes. Their ability should help them understand how sensing themes is the first step in using a systematic, disciplined way of analyzing (i.e., encoding) information, whether the information is verbal, behavioral, documented, or live. The book should help readers become sensitive to some of the research design issues, such as sampling and establishing interrater reliability, that can contribute to the effectiveness of thematic analysis or render it a futile exercise. The book should be useful for people developing codes, whether in the discovery phase or the hypothesis-testing phase of their inquiry. Although the primary focus is for people planning to develop new codes, the book should also be helpful for those people intending to use an existing code in their research.

The Intended Audience

The primary audience is intended to be graduate students and young professionals in the social sciences, in particular the applied behavioral sciences, such as psychology, social psychology, sociology, cultural anthropology, or any of the applied combinations of the above basic disciplines to fields and professions such as management, organizational behavior, social work, nursing, dentistry, medicine, law, or education. A secondary audience could be students enrolled in research methods courses at any level in the above-named fields.

A caution, however, for those prospective readers who are self-proclaimed quantiphobes or qualiphobes. If you are a qualiphobe, this book will not convince you of the legitimacy of qualitative methods. If you are a quantiphobe, this book will not convince you of the importance of scoring, scaling, and clustering to allow for the translation of qualitative information into a format amenable to statistical analysis. The book is offered for those who want to explore or learn how to expand the variety of processes and methods useful in their research. It is for the curious.

Future manuscripts may be workbooks or CD-ROM versions, providing numerous exercises for the full development of thematic analysis capability. This book provides several in-depth examples that can be used as exercises, notably in Chapters 1 (with dream analysis), 4 (with analysis of life stories) and 5 (with analysis of a critical incident interview). The reader with a concrete-experience and/or active experimental learning style who is attempting to develop the skills and techniques of thematic analysis may want to use these examples as exercises. All of the needed materials are provided. The first potential exercise in Chapter 1 may take an hour or so. The second potential exercise in Chapter 4 may take 3 to 5 hours. The third potential exercise in Chapter 5 may take an hour or two. The reader with an abstract-conceptualization learning style may want to skip these lengthy examples and return to them when he or she feels the need.

Numerous brief examples are provided throughout the book to illustrate points. These examples are drawn from a wide spectrum of colleagues' and my own work with thematic analysis on a variety of types of information and research in various fields or disciplines. A number of lengthy examples are also provided to illustrate details and complexity of the method and its design components, such as analysis of the aggressive behavior of men while drinking alcoholic beverages (and the degree of prosocial behavior evident), comparison of life stories of superior-performing managers of scientists and engineers and their less effective counterparts, analysis of critical incidents from the work of a systems designer who is supervising an information systems department in a company, and coding of the interpersonal sensitivity demonstrated by graduate students for developmental feedback in a professional program. Although several of these lengthy examples are drawn from my own work in the last 15 years in organizational behavior and the social psychology of people in management, it is hoped that readers can be flexible and make the conceptual leap to the forms and types of qualitative information involved in their research and fields. Future editions or other manuscripts may offer field- and discipline-specific, in-depth illustrations, but it was too daunting a task for this book!

An Outline

Chapter 1 introduces the process of thematic analysis and describes the many different types of research and research methods with which it may be useful.

The following ideas are briefly reviewed in the chapter: the concept of the codable moment; the steps in developing the abilities to use thematic analysis; the scope of the types of information on which it can be used; the major threats to its appropriate use; the difference between manifest and latent analysis; the major sources of error in the use of thematic analysis, such as projection, fatigue, boredom, sampling, familiarity, and lack of familiarity, and how to minimize their impact on the collection of your raw information; the categorization and classification process; and interpretation.

As an introductory exercise in using thematic analysis, four dreams are offered, two from Carl Jung and two from Robert Louis Stevenson. The reader is invited to analyze the dreams for manifest- as well as latent-content themes. Analysis of the dreams is followed by a brief review of the two dreamers' lives. The biographical sketches illustrate how even rudimentary manifest and latent analysis can provide insights and description of themes in a person's life.

Chapter 2 describes the process of developing and using themes and codes. There are primarily three approaches to developing themes systematically: (a) theory driven, (b) prior data or prior research driven, and (c) inductive. Each of these approaches is discussed. Particular emphasis is given to the inductive method, not because it is better than the others, but for two reasons: (a) The inductive method provides the most fundamental method of developing themes and a code, and (b) it is the least frequently used process for developing themes and probably the least understood. The three steps for generating a code deductively from theory or prior research and the five steps in developing a code from raw information are described.

A good code is one that captures the qualitative richness of the phenomenon. A good code may emerge from one or more original themes. Once it is developed as a code, it becomes the form of the original themes that the researcher uses throughout his or her inquiry. It is usable in the analysis, interpretation, and presentation of the research. From the perspective of scoring and scaling for quantitative analysis, a good code will also have the maximum probability of producing high interrater reliability and validity. A good code should have five elements:

1. A label
2. A definition of what the theme concerns (i.e., the characteristic or issue constituting the theme)
3. A description of how to know when the theme occurs (i.e., how to "flag" the theme)

4. A description of any qualifications or exclusions to the identification of the theme

5. Examples, both positive and negative, to eliminate possible confusion when looking for the theme

Because the development of thematic codes is particularly sensitive to contaminants in the original information, sampling is a key step in the research process. Beyond the usual concerns of generalizing from a sample to a population, sampling decisions will affect thematic analysis in the consistency or reliability of judgments attainable. Because qualitative methods are often used in early stages of inquiry and to examine unusual or complex phenomena, the degree to which the raw information represents the phenomenon becomes an interpretive dilemma requiring theoretical as well as empirical support or justification for the sample studied.

Chapter 3 addresses issues of sampling. In addition to typical research concerns about sampling, thematic analysis requires distinctions as to the sampling of the units of coding and sampling of the units of analysis. Because this affects the nature and quality of the themes observed and code developed, it is crucial to understand the decisions the researcher will make at this point. The unit of analysis is the entity on which the interpretation of the study will focus. The unit of coding is the most basic segment, or element, of the raw data or information that can be assessed in a meaningful way regarding the phenomenon. The chapter discusses of the costs and benefits of various units of coding as applied to different sources of raw information, such as thought samples (e.g., Thematic Apperception Test stories or life histories), behavior (e.g., critical incident interviews, videotaped behavior, transcripts of conversations), interaction (e.g., videotaped group situations), and historical documents (e.g., previously recorded information such as songs, memos, speeches, newspapers, or myths).

For example, the sampling design of research studies using thematic analysis should be tested as to its adequacy and appropriateness with regard to its efficacy, efficiency, and ethics. Efficacy is addressed through questions such as: (a) Is there sufficient variety of types of *units of analysis* to allow for analysis of "between-unit" variation or differences, and therefore generalization? and (b) Is there sufficient variety of types of *units of coding* to allow for a comprehensive understanding and analysis of the unit of analysis?

Efficiency becomes a vital ingredient in the sampling aspect of the research design. In thematic analysis, as in any form of qualitative analysis, the time requirements grow in a multiplicative manner beyond the time to view the videotapes or read essays or watch live interaction.

The raw data or information collected for studies using thematic analysis is a person's own words or actions or observable aspects of his or her life in an organization or culture. This often results in relatively more "sensitive" raw data than are usually obtained from questionnaires or surveys. The increased sensitivity requires a high degree of thought and caution regarding the subject's informed consent, protection of confidentiality, protection against abusive use of raw or coded data, and protection against abusive application of the results of the study.

Chapters 4 and 5 provide examples of thematic analysis in action that can serve as exercises. Each chapter contains raw information that the reader can use to develop and apply a thematic code. In Chapter 4, six life stories collected during a research project of highly effective middle-level managers of a research and development facility and their less effective counterparts are presented. The reader is guided through each of the five steps described in Chapter 2 of inductively developing a thematic code. The results of the study from which these autobiographies were drawn are then reviewed to illustrate the latter steps of the process.

In Chapter 5, the process of applying a code developed in prior research is described with an example from a critical incident interview. This chapter approaches thematic analysis with the assumption that the researcher is planning to use someone else's thematic code or an existing code. The reader is guided through each of the three steps described in Chapter 2 of deductively generating a thematic code.

Once the researcher has developed a code or identified themes, he or she can use the information with a wide range of modes and methods of analysis. These methods can be seen as lying on a continuum. At the one end is an exclusively qualitative and verbally descriptive approach to the phenomenon under investigation; at the other end is a primarily quantitative approach of statistically analyzing the phenomenon. Points along the continuum may be quantitative description of the frequency of themes shown and other mixtures of methods.

Once the themes have been identified, but before further analysis and interpretation, issues of scoring, scaling, clustering, and reliability of judgment must be addressed. Chapter 6 addresses the issues of how to score the themes identified. It discusses possible approaches to creating scales and clusters of themes as ways to organize the "code."

The topic of reliability, more than any other aspect of qualitative research methods, evokes philosophical debate on the merits of positivist versus postmodernist approaches to "science." *Inquiry* becomes a code word for declarations of casting off the shackles of assumptions and criteria of quality from other sciences (other than the social or behavioral sciences). Although some researchers simply choose to discard the concept of reliability as tainted with positivist, universalist "bad values," Chapter 7 discusses ideas as to why and how to consider the need for consistency of judgment in qualitative research.

Converting themes into codes and then counting presence, frequency, or intensity does not in and of itself create a link between qualitative and quantitative methods. The computation or articulation of interrater reliability, or convergence of perception of multiple judges, must occur as well. As described by Creswell (1994) and discovered by most of us, the linkage is desirable because it allows researchers to combine the richness and uniqueness of qualitative information and the precision and discipline of quantitative methods. Returning to the analogy of people meeting for the first time who speak different languages, with reliability as consistency of judgment, thematic analysis provides for methodological translation and conceptual bridges between two or more approaches to discovery.

Positivist social science and interpretive social science can be viewed as two substantially different paradigms (Silverman, 1993). Thematic analysis allows the interpretive social scientist's social construction of meaning to be articulated or packaged in such a way, with reliability as consistency of judgment, that description of social "facts" or observations seems to emerge. The identification of these observations satisfies the positivist social scientist's conceptual definition of discovery. The reverse process can help the interpretive social scientist understand the special and distinctive qualities of observations made by the positivist social scientist through thematic analysis.

Thematic analysis with reliability also allows the interpretive social scientist to generate qualitative hypotheses that provide a basis for a positivist social scientist to conduct qualitative or quantitative hypothesis testing as part of the building process of science. Whether you call this combination of methods a conceptual bridge or a Satanic perversion, it begs for new labels. Miller and Crabtree (1992) went so far as to call it qualitative positivism. Thematic analysis also allows the opposite process. The hypothesis testing of a positivist social scientist can be viewed as producing observations or themes that the interpretive social scientist can then use for exploration.

Regardless of ontology or epistemology, a code or codebook and assessment of consistency of observation provide (a) reliability for the positivist or postpositivist; (b) dependability for the postmodernist; (c) ability to communicate with others (i.e., to engage in social construction) for the hermeneutic, interactionist, or relativist; and/or (d) ability to interact with others about observations (i.e., dialogue or conversation) to the relationist.

Various approaches to defining consistency of judgment are discussed in Chapter 7. Different types of reliability are discussed as appropriate to different types of raw information and various coding schemes.

The book ends with a few thoughts about the challenges ahead to researchers. Current obstacles faced by researchers seeking to use thematic analysis are

1. Helping people to "see"—that is, helping researchers and scholars to break out of frames and assumptions about legitimate sources of information and to open their eyes to the richness of information around them every day
2. Helping transform the qualitative-versus-quantitative debate in research methods into a challenge to blend creativity and ingenuity of observers and researchers
3. Helping researchers, observers, and practitioners to develop skills in code development and to appreciate the importance of reliability in using and applying thematic codes
4. Helping to create an environment for collaborative research where thematic analysis can be conducted appropriately

Sensing Themes in Research: A Personal Path

It is important to understand an author's "context" when reading. As a way to help the reader perceive my intellectual context and the variety of fields and types of information with which I have come to understand and value thematic analysis, I offer the path of my intellectual history related to my research. Many people and their ideas have influenced my approach to research and the important role that thematic analysis has played in it. This account of the intellectual path on which I have traveled may help the reader to appreciate, or at least tolerate, what may at times seem like discontinuous jumps of logic, faith, or loss of disciplinary focus.

My introduction to thematic analysis was part of a transition from aeronautics and astronautics into social and behavioral sciences. In 1967, I joined David A. Kolb in using techniques developed by David C. McClelland, John W. Atkinson, and Joseph Veroff to analyze the motivational imagery in Thematic Apperception Tests. This led me to study the use of thematic methods of interpretation in the study of personality by Henry Murray and William James and eventually in the motivational research of Elizabeth French, Matina Horner, and David G. Winter.

The initial challenge to develop codes occurred in the same research project when David Kolb and I wished to build on his earlier work with David Berlew, Sara Winter, and others in understanding self-directed behavior change. We developed thematic codes to analyze and then interpret people's essays describing their current and desired self-image.

I was pulled into thematic analysis as if by a strong current. I used thematic analysis first with interviews regarding adult socialization for Edgar Schein and then with analysis of psychohistorical patterns in people's childhood as precursors to adult behavior for Everett Hagen. In the following year, I was using thematic codes with folktales and myths of numerous cultures around the world through the Human Relations Area Files at Harvard for John and Bea Whiting and with interpersonal interaction among people in small groups for Freed Bales. My doctoral education was an alternating sequence of immersion in theory, research discoveries, thematic analysis of various forms of qualitative information, and then formal quantitative ways to analyze all of this information.

First in the field of personality and then in the fields of adult development and clinical psychology, sociology, cultural anthropology, and social psychology, I was engaged in thematic analysis of people's thoughts, behavior, interactions, or records of individual and collective behavior (i.e., folktales).

Following completion of my doctoral work, the path continued with my "coding" of literature and political speeches on the basis of David McClelland's and David Winter's methods and my exploration of biodata and life histories with Charles Dailey, cognitive complexity with Abigail Stewart, and intrapersonal focus with James Burruss. The application of these methods and development of new variations, codes, and information collection techniques continued in my work with colleagues at McBer and Company. First, I used the methods on antecedents and consequences of alcohol consumption on aggressive behavior and therapeutic programs for alcoholics. Later, I applied the methods to topics of managerial competency analysis (with Lyle Spencer, Murray Dalziel, and others), organizational climate (with Steve Williamson), management and executive development, career development and planning, and human resource and organization development.

A number of years later, I moved from research and consulting into an academic role at Case Western Reserve University. As a professor of organizational behavior, I felt compelled to help doctoral students wrestling with research projects and dissertations using qualitative information. In much the same way as David McClelland at Harvard and Boston University, Abigail Stewart and David Winter at the University of Michigan, and others have responded to their students' needs, I developed a doctoral seminar in 1987 and have offered it every year. This book has grown out of the experiences and materials used in this course.

Acknowledgments

Insight and the research that produces or yields the insight is not the product of one person, one mind, or one heart. It both takes many people and is a reflection of many people. First, and above all, I wish to thank my wife, Sandy, for all of her patience with my all-too-often preoccupied thoughts, her forgiveness for disrupted weekends and ruined evenings, her insight into human nature, and her gift to me of the spirit and love to explore and write. Many friends and colleagues have provided encouragement for the development and continual improvement of the doctoral seminar on which this book is based and the writing of the book, not to mention providing editorial feedback along the way. Thank you: Mitch Allen, Lisa Berlinger, Barbara Bird, Diana Bilimoria, Chris J. Boyatzis, Susan S. Case, David Cooperrider, Scott S. Cowen, Christine Dreyfus, Vanessa Druskat, Cindy Forman, Ron Fry, Retta Holdorf, David A. Kolb, Peter LaBella, David C. McClelland, Annie McKee, Angela Murphy, Eric Neilsen, William Pasmore, Franco Ratti, Ken Rhee, Lyle M. Spencer, Jr., Suresh Srivastva, Jane Wheeler, Judith White, Helen Williams, David G. Winter, Don Wolfe, and Rob Wright.

CHAPTER ONE

The Search for
the Codable Moment

A Way of Seeing

Thematic analysis is a way of seeing. Often, what one sees through thematic analysis does not appear to others, even if they are observing the same information, events, or situations. To others, if they agree with the insight, the insight appears almost magical. If they are empowered by the insight, it appears visionary. If they disagree with the insight, it appears delusionary. Observation precedes understanding. Recognizing an important moment (seeing) precedes encoding it (seeing it as something), which in turn precedes interpretation. Thematic analysis moves you through these three phases of inquiry.

Sensing Themes in Life

> The officer lingers in an alleyway a moment to check for fresh graffiti. The scrawling and their proximity to rival turf tell him much about tensions, who's who in a gang, and coming events in Lennox, the birthplace of the most powerful of black gangs, the Crips. ("How Deputy Stresses Brains, 1988, p. A8)

Herb Giron, a Deputy Sheriff in Lennox, California, near Los Angeles, used thematic analysis of graffiti and the rhythm of the street to anticipate events. He stressed information gathering. While driving through town conducting various duties, he would stop to talk with people in the streets. He talked to people known and not known as gang members and to victims of past gang violence.

In the Kalahari, the people of the !Kung society use thematic analysis to track animals. Considered among the world's best trackers, they learn it over many years. When they use the skill, it appears effortless.

> The !Kung hunter can deduce many kinds of information about the animal he is tracking: its species and sex, its age, how fast it is traveling, whether it is alone or with other animals, its physical condition (healthy or ill), whether and on what it is feeding, and the time of day the animal passed this way. The species, of course, is identified by the shape of the hoofprint and by the dung or scat. . . . The size or age of an animal correlates directly with the size of its print. The depth of the print indicates the weight of the animal. An ill or infirm animal may be distinguished by a halting gait or uneven stride length. . . . Knowledge of the animal's habits aids in determining the time of day it passed by. . . . If the tracks zigzag from shade tree to tree, the animal went through the heat of the day. If the tracks go under the west side of the trees, the animal was catching the morning shade. . . . Milling tracks within a small radius out in the open suggest that the animal was there at night and was sleeping. . . . When fresh, the print is clean-cut, but after an hour (or less, if the day is windy) a fine covering of windblown sand collects in the depression. Later, twigs and grass fall in, and then insect and other animal tracks are superimposed. The moisture content of the soil 1, 2, 3, or 4 centimeters below the surface and the rate at which soil dries out after being exposed by a footfall are two variables that are exceedingly well studied by the !Kung. (Lee, 1979, pp. 47-48)

To the uninitiated, the tracking skill of the !Kung seems magical. A thoughtful observer may use words like "natural" or "intuitive" to describe the capability of the tracker. To those of us who do not spend hours studying animals in the bush, it appears to be an effortless process and the exercise of a capability with unconscious ease. It does not seem to be the deliberate exercise of a skill or process of analysis.

People using thematic analysis may appear to be making the observations and coming to the insights "intuitively." For them, the use of the process of analysis has become unconscious, much as multiplying single digits is for many people.

Franklin Pensato, president of a Fortune 500 chemical manufacturing company (the name has been changed to protect his confidentiality), assessed the atmosphere inside the company during his first 4 months as company president. Although he had been a president of one of the company's divisions for a number of years, he had not thought carefully about the internal atmosphere. The climate of the entire company was a function of the climate in each of the divisions. It was 1983. His reading of the national and international economic situation was that he had a few years of prosperity to get things in good shape before the next cyclical downturn hit his company. As he listened to briefings from each of the divisional presidents, met with their staff, and discussed issues with people in the various functions, Franklin was disturbed. Each of the divisions saw the other divisions as different companies. Although they shared various resources, such as manufacturing plants, an R&D center, and certain staff functions, the perception of difference seemed to lead to a sense of competition with other divisions regarding various resources. This type of envy appeared to exist even within the various divisions and to affect interdepartmental and interfunctional workings.

As he listened to the analysis of the future trends in each business, Franklin sensed and then concluded that each type of business needed its own autonomy: its own strategy, its own structure, and its own organizational climate. He decided to start with a detailed study of each business area, not defined by divisions or simply by markets or technologies. The result was the development of significantly different approaches to managing and leading each of the basically different businesses. He viewed the linking of strategy and structure to the creation of a climate appropriate to the future needs of each business—not the past needs. Franklin Pensato was using thematic analysis to "read" the internal climate of the organization and its divisions. It helped him and other executives to discover new strategic agendas for each of the various businesses.

Finding a Codable Moment

In each of these examples, people used thematic analysis to see something that had not been evident to others. They perceived a pattern, or theme, in seemingly random information.

They saw a pattern! The perception of this pattern begins the process of thematic analysis. It allows these people to continue to the next major step, classifying or encoding the pattern. They give it a label or definition or description. This allows them to proceed to the third major step in thematic analysis, interpreting the pattern.

If sensing a pattern or "occurrence" can be called *seeing,* then the encoding of it can be called *seeing as.* That is, you first make the observation that something important or notable is occurring, and then you classify or describe it. In the way that Wittgenstein (Creegan, 1989) described the process by which we classify experiences in our lives, the *seeing as* provides us with a link between a new or emergent pattern and any and all patterns that we have observed and considered previously. It also provides a link to any and all patterns that others have observed and considered previously through reading.

It all begins with capturing the codable moment. But before we get too far into the details of the process, additional discussion of the overall purpose will set the stage.

What Is Thematic Analysis?

Thematic analysis is a process to be used with qualitative information. It is not another qualitative method but a process that can be used with most, if not all, qualitative methods *and* that allows for the translation of qualitative information into quantitative data, if this is desired by the researcher.

Thematic analysis is a process for encoding qualitative information. The encoding requires an explicit "code." This may be a list of themes; a complex model with themes, indicators, and qualifications that are causally related; or something in between these two forms. A theme is a pattern found in the information that at minimum describes and organizes the possible observations and at maximum interprets aspects of the phenomenon. A theme may be identified at the manifest level (directly observable in the information) or at the latent level (underlying the phenomenon). The themes may be initially generated inductively from the raw information or generated deductively from theory and prior research. The compilation or integration of a number of codes in a study is often called a *codebook.*

Thematic analysis has a number of overlapping or alternate purposes. It can be used as

1. A way of *seeing*
2. A way of *making sense* out of seemingly unrelated material
3. A way of *analyzing* qualitative information

4. A way of *systematically observing* a person, an interaction, a group, a situation, an organization, or a culture

5. A way of *converting* qualitative information into quantitative data

Thematic analysis enables scholars, observers, or practitioners to use a wide variety of types of information in a systematic manner that increases their accuracy or sensitivity in understanding and interpreting observations about people, events, situations, and organizations. Coffey and Atkinson (1996) stated, "Coding can be thought about as a way of relating our data to our ideas about these data" (p. 27). They emphasized that coding provides many benefits in the organization, processing, and analysis of qualitative information. A code is not necessarily, in their view, a conceptual scheme. The interpretation phase of research follows development and use of a thematic code.

Although researchers may find thematic analysis to be of most use in the early stages of the research inquiry process, such as the pilot stage, it can be useful at all stages. During the prediscovery, "fuzzy" stage of formulation of a research agenda, thematic analysis enables the researcher to access a wide variety of phenomenological information as an inductive beginning of the inquiry.

Every day, we encounter, observe, and then pass by numerous sources of information or "data" useful in gaining insight about phenomena of interest to us in the world. The anticipation of the frustration of not knowing how to access the information often limits observers' or scholars' further exploration. Thematic analysis opens the doors to many of these forms of information and guides the observer or scholar to their possible use.

For the scholar, thematic analysis allows the collection or use of qualitative information in a manner facilitating communication with a broad audience of other scholars or researchers. To make results from qualitative research accessible to others, one must employ different ways of organizing and presenting them (Miles & Huberman, 1984). Often, researchers using quantitative and qualitative methodologies battle on the level of philosophical abstractions merely because they are having difficulty communicating with each other. People will vigorously argue about their differing epistemologies—differing ways of knowing—and will engage in defensive derogation of others' methods. Thematic analysis offers a vehicle for increasing communication in ways that researchers using various methods can appreciate. These methods have been enhanced by the use of computers for thoughtful documentation and analysis of qualitative information (Weitzman & Miles, 1995).

Thematic analysis is regularly used by scholars and researchers in literature, psychology, sociology, cultural anthropology, history, art, political science, economics, mathematics, chemistry, physics, biology, astronomy, and many other fields (Crabtree & Miller, 1992; Denzin & Lincoln, 1994; Marshall & Rossman, 1989; Silverman, 1993). Often it is used without being specifically described, and it may be referred to by many different names. Scholars in the latter-named fields in the above list often use thematic analysis to identify quantitative patterns and develop appropriate codes. Scholars in the earlier-named fields in the above list often use thematic analysis to identify verbal or visual patterns and develop appropriate codes.

For example, a management consultant uses thematic analysis to analyze new market trends, a company's desired strategy, or corporate culture. A clinical psychologist or psychiatrist uses thematic analysis to understand his or her patient, whether an individual, family, or group, and to determine what intervention would be most useful.

Miller and Crabtree (1992) offered a typology of various domains and traditions of qualitative research (see Table 1.1). As the table shows, thematic analysis can be used by a researcher in any of these "traditions" to process, analyze, and/or interpret his or her information, regardless of his or her ontology or epistemology.

Thematic analysis can be a beneficial bridge between researchers of varying orientations and fields (Denzin & Lincoln, 1994; Miller & Crabtree, 1992). It allows a researcher using a qualitative method to more easily communicate his or her observations, findings, and interpretation of meaning to others who are using different methods. This increased ability to communicate allows more comprehensive understanding of the phenomenon. It may provide crucial insights to scholars in their review of "what is known" to guide their research strategy and design. Often, various methods contribute different insights in the quest to understand a phenomenon.

If a researcher wishes to attempt bridging, or translating his or her methods and results into forms accessible to others from different fields, orientations, or traditions of inquiry, thematic analysis can assist in communication between positivistic science and interpretive science, between testers of ideas and developers of ideas, between builders of theories and social constructionists, suggesting that theory builds itself anew with each setting (Silverman, 1993). A major challenge in the social sciences and in particular the behavioral sciences has been overcoming epistemological chauvinism

TABLE 1.1 Miller and Crabtree's (1992) Domains of Study and Qualitative Research Traditions

Domain	Research Tradition
Lived experience ("lifeworld")	Psychology
Intention of actor as individual	Phenomenology
Actors as access to social context	Hermeneutics (interpretive interactionism)
Individual	Psychology and anthropology
As person with biography	Life history (interpretive biography)
Behavior/events	Psychology
Over time and in context	Ethology
Related to environment	Ecological psychology
Social world	Sociology
How individuals achieve shared agreement	Ethnomethodology
How humans create and interact in a symbolic environment	Symbolic interaction (semiotics)
General relations among social categories and properties	Grounded theory
Culture	Anthropology
As holistic whole	Ethnography
As symbolic world	Symbolic anthropology
As cognitive map of social organizations shared meanings, and semantic rules	Ethnoscience (cognitive anthropology)
Communication/talk	Sociolinguistics
Forms and mechanisms of actual conversation	Conversation analysis (Discourse analysis)
Forms and mechanism of nonverbal communication	Kinesics/proxemics
Patterns and rules of communication	Ethnography of communication
Practice and Process	Applied professions
Caring	Nursing research
Teaching and learning	Educational research
Managing/consuming	Organizational/market research
Evaluation	Evaluation research

SOURCE: From Crabtree and Miller (1992, p. 24).

and using all methods to enrich our understanding of human phenomena (Campbell, 1988).

The Ability to See

The ability to use thematic analysis appears to involve a number of underlying abilities, or competencies. One competency can be called *pattern recognition.* It is the ability to see patterns in seemingly random information. As Strauss and Corbin (1990) indicated, the researcher must also have an *openness* and *flexibility* (i.e., conceptual flexibility) to perceive the patterns. Further, this openness must be sustainable. Typically, research using qualitative methods requires long hours of immersion in information collection and even more hours in information processing and analysis before interpretation.

Another pair of competencies involved are *planning* and *systems thinking*. They enable a person to organize his or her observations and identified patterns into a *usable system* for observation (i.e., that others can use or that the person can use consistently at other times).

Knowledge relevant to the arena being examined is crucial as a foundation, often referred to as tacit *knowledge*. For example, it is difficult to perceive and make sense of patterns in Shakespeare without understanding Greek and Roman mythology. Strauss and Corbin (1990) claimed that "theoretical sensitivity" is the ability of the researcher to recognize what is important, give it meaning, and conceptualize the observations. In this sense, a researcher needs to have the patience to perceive themes or patterns and the "lens" through which to view them. Cleaning your glasses helps, but conducting qualitative research involves emotional, value-laden, and theoretical preconceptions, preferences, and worldviews.

Other abilities or competencies may be relevant and necessary to using thematic analysis with specific types of information, such as the aural skills to perceive patterns in symphonies. With certain sources of information, other competencies, such as empathy and social objectivity, may be crucial and are relevant to perceiving patterns in a person's life.

Although training and education can increase a person's skill and precision or discipline in using thematic analysis, the underlying capabilities mentioned above can be found in people in many occupations and all cultures, social classes, ages, genders, races, and ethnoreligious groups. What seems intuitive, natural, or almost magical to the untrained can be understood, on observation and deconstruction, as a set of capabilities. Because the capabilities involve perception and analytic reasoning, it is believed that they can be developed. The length of time and study may differ from person to person. Probably, individual differences in the above-mentioned capabilities will affect the time and duration of study required to refine the ability to perform thematic analysis.

Cognitive complexity appears to be the only prerequisite for using thematic analysis. Cognitive complexity involves perceiving multiple causality and multiple variables over time and other variations, as well as the ability to conceptualize a system of relationships. Components of cognitive complexity were described in the thematic code reported by Winter and McClelland (1978). In studying advanced forms of compare-and-contrast analysis among liberal arts students, they identified six processes that helped in generating themes: direct compound comparative statements; description of exceptions and qualifications to an element or dichotomy; citation of examples from the source material; identification of an overarching issue organizing multiple themes or dichotomies; willingness to redefine a theme to address more of the source information; and subsuming of alternatives appearing as functional equivalents. They identified three processes that hindered the generation of themes: "apples and oranges" comparison of nonequivalencies; affect projected by the analyzer as a dichotomy; and personalized differential reactions projected as dichotomies. Miles and Huberman (1984) discussed the importance of the researcher's ability to "cluster" perceived themes in order to move to higher levels of abstraction. Whether entirely learned or learned within boundaries genetically determined, cognitive complexity is not the same as the form of intellectual ability measured by IQ tests and similar standardized tests that are often called cognitive ability tests. These tests assess only one form of cognitive complexity and are significantly affected by language, socialization, culture, and social class.

Developing the Ability

The ability to use thematic analysis appears to have four distinct stages in its development. In the first stage, the researcher must be able to "sense themes": that is, to recognize a codable moment. Professionals can be trained to sense themes and develop the ability to use thematic analysis. People often use the metaphor of establishing the best "focal length" as a way to discuss sensing themes. When you look at a phenomenon or a person or material, what is the best distance to hold it from your eyes? What distance allows you to see the themes and patterns clearly? Books and articles about chaos theory and fractals have given ample evidence of the difference between seeing patterns or not as a function of focal length. A lengthy example (that can be used as an exercise) in sensing themes is offered later in this chapter in analyzing dreams.

To sense themes or to begin the process of developing codes, researchers must be open to all information. All of their senses should be ready to receive pertinent information. It helps if the raw information has been recorded with minimal or no processing. It also helps if the researcher has a grounding or training in the fundamentals and concepts of the fields relevant to the inquiry.

This provides some insight about where to look and what to look for—or, more accurately, what to be ready to "see."

In the second stage, researchers must train or discipline themselves to use themes, or codes, reliably. The second stage is the ability "to see" and "to see as" (i.e., to recognize the codable moment and encode it) *consistently.* Consistency in your own judgments is important. If you looked at the same event today and tomorrow, would you see it and encode it in the same or a similar way? Another form of consistency is measured by the degree to which others (i.e., other trained researchers) would see it and encode it the same or a similar way. In other words, the perception and coding do not merely reflect your idiosyncratic view of the world.

Although the issue of reliability will often evoke epistemological or philosophical arguments from qualitative researchers, the reader is asked to suspend any such immediate reaction and to consider the concepts and justification offered for being concerned about consistency of judgment. A longer discussion of the various epistemological perspectives involved appears in Chapter 7.

It helps to have excitement and an interest in the code or in the raw information being examined. Researchers can learn to overcome their tendencies to project, such as imposing or reading into the raw information their own values, thoughts, feelings, and competencies. This can be accomplished with disciplined observation and attention to detail. They can also learn to minimize the impact of transference, such as "halo" or "villain" effects. These issues will be discussed later in this chapter. Researchers have commented that it helps, at this point in developing the skills in thematic analysis, to memorize the code being used. Such memorizing frees the researcher to read the information and not be preoccupied with continually scanning the code.

Over years of training doctoral students in thematic analysis and code development, my colleagues and I have observed that learning to apply other researchers' thematic codes reliably is helpful to the researcher. It aids him or her in developing the discipline of consistent observation within a context or particular study. It also develops the researcher's sensitivity to aspects of a thematic code that make it easier or more difficult to use. A little training at this stage saves future researchers (who may want to use your code) hundreds of hours of anguish in trying to learn it. It may be critical to the future use of your code by others: If your code is too difficult to learn, other researchers will avoid it, and the field will lose the benefit of building on your work directly.

In the third stage of learning thematic analysis, researchers must develop a code to process and analyze or capture the essence of their observations. The qualitative information offers a feast of insights. It is the challenge to the researcher to find and use them well. Though researchers need to immerse themselves in the information to appreciate its richness, various steps in the process are aided by discussing multiple views and perceptions of the same information. The code development process is typically better when it is done with others.

As in the first two stages of developing thematic analysis, openness to information and discipline are essential in developing codes. In the third stage, the skill is primarily developed and refined through practice, practice, and more practice. Once a researcher has developed three or four codes for different studies and various types of raw information, he or she will typically become adept at code development.

In the fourth stage, the researcher must interpret the information and themes in a way that contributes to the development of knowledge. This will require some theory or conceptual framework. The theory may have been developed from the literature in a traditional sequence of research or may emerge from the information being analyzed, as in grounded theory development. In addition, communication of the "meaning" of the findings, observations, or results may require translation into a format accessible to other researchers. Often, this involves some form of presentation or display appropriate for qualitative information (Miles & Huberman, 1984). It may also involve a conversion into quantitative data, which is easily done through thematic analysis.

To summarize, the four stages in developing the ability to use thematic analysis are

1. *Sensing themes*—that is, recognizing the codable moment
2. *Doing it reliably*—that is, recognizing the codable moment and encoding it consistently·
3. *Developing codes*
4. *Interpreting the information and themes in the context of a theory or conceptual framework*—that is, contributing to the development of knowledge

The stages of learning thematic analysis follow a sequence similar to that of learning a new language. In experiential learning theory, Kolb (1984) contended that apprehension precedes comprehension, which then feeds into further apprehension, and so the cycle continues. Often, in learning a language, a person first must apprehend the sights—that is, the formations of the alphabet of the language and its sounds. This is similar to sensing themes and/or recognizing the codable moment. Next, a person learns to comprehend the language through reading and listening. This is similar to the challenge of consistency in recognizing the codable moment and encoding it reliably. The more difficult challenge of writing in the new language often emerges following prolonged practice with reading and listening to it. This is similar to the developing of codes. A person is composing and constructing with the new language in the same way that a researcher is constructing an interpretation of events and observations with a thematic code.

The last development in learning a new language is speaking it. This requires interaction with others. To improve in this stage often requires interacting with native speakers of the language. This is similar to the challenges of interpreting the meaning of the discoveries or observations made through the use of the thematic code. Contribution to knowledge requires interaction with others, either in the development of the interpretation or in the reading of it and building on it in future research, appreciation, or critique.

Types of Raw Information and Phenomena

As mentioned earlier in this chapter, thematic analysis allows the researcher to use a wide variety of information. Thematic analysis can be used with thought samples from projective tests, life histories, or open-ended essays; behavior samples from interviews, videotaped encounters, simulations, transcripts of speeches, memos, personal letters, or personal diaries; interactions from videotapes, audiotapes, or transcripts of conversations; and historical documents, such as songs, literature, folktales, hymns, children's readers, art, films, memos, and personal letters (Winter, 1992).

Major Obstacles to Effective Thematic Analysis

There are three major obstacles or threats to using thematic analysis effectively in research. They are the researcher's (a) projection, (b) sampling, and (c) mood and style. For the novice or experienced researcher using thematic analysis, there are actions to take when encountering any of these major obstacles. Many of these "actions" should be thought of as preventive measures rather than antidotes to be taken once the disease is contracted!

Projection

Projection is one of our ego defense mechanisms (Freud, 1936/1966; Valliant, 1992). It helps us interact with others, but it can also become an obstacle to effective and insightful thematic analysis. It is simply "reading into" or "attributing to" another person something that is your own characteristic, emotion, value, attitude, or such. With ambiguous qualitative information, there is more opportunity for and invitation to projection from the researcher than in most other types of research. The stronger a researcher's ideology or theory, the more he or she will be tempted to project his or her values or conceptualization of the events onto the people from whom the raw information has been collected.

Familiarity with the phenomenon being studied and the source material, such as setting and type of qualitative information being collected, has a curvilinear relationship with encouraging projection. When researchers have too much familiarity, it is often difficult for them to resist their own typical response to the situation. A researchers easily finds him- or herself saying, "Well, if I were in their place, I would have meant to say. . . ." Similarly, researchers with no or little familiarity with a phenomenon tend to direct their attention to the manifest level. The novelty of the situation can be overwhelming, especially when one is using live or videotaped material. Appropriate levels of familiarity allow *useful* projection, such as saying to oneself, "I understand their language," but not projection to the degree that the researcher "fills in" the blanks or ambiguous moments.

Preventing or lessening the contamination of projection is helped by (a) developing an explicit code; (b) establishing consistency of judgment—that is, reliability; (c) using several people to encode the information and a diversity of perspectives—perhaps even by having the participants (i.e., subjects) examine the raw information themselves; and (d) sticking close to the raw information in the development of the themes and code. The researcher is also helped if he or she practices being open to sensing themes and interpreting them in a wide range of types of source material. A willingness to examine a prevailing theory and to test its assumptions is often a foundation for the openness needed. Of course, the best technique for minimizing the effect of projection is to practice, practice, and practice thematic analysis and code development.

The theme of the importance and difficulty of developing consistency of judgment, or reliability, can be found in film and literature. The complexity and richness of different perspectives on the same events were explored in Akira Kurosawa's 1951 Japanese film *Rashomon,* a story of a violent rape-murder from the views of four people involved. Similarly, Lawrence Durrell's *Alexandria Quartet,* consisting of four novels, *Justine, Balthazar, Mountolive,* and *Clea,* first published between 1957 and 1960, tells a love story involving an intertwined set of relationships during a tormented period from four different perspectives; three of the novels view and tell about the same events, and the fourth constitutes a sequel. Durrell's (1961) own note at the beginning of *Balthazar* states that "three sides of space and one of time constitute the soup-mix recipe of a continuum" (p. 1). The challenge to the qualitative researcher is to use thematic analysis to draw the richness of the themes from the raw information without reducing the insights to a trivial level for the sake of consistency of judgment.

Sampling

When you are using thematic analysis with any form of qualitative analysis, the law of "garbage in, garbage out" applies. If the raw information that you are processing and analyzing is full of contamination from factors or variables about which you are not aware, your analysis and therefore any subsequent interpretation is doomed. Before assessing consistency of judgment, sensing themes, and developing a code, before validating your observations in whatever form is appropriate to your design, there is the problem of sampling.

If you want to develop a thematic analysis of what people in the United States are thinking about when they are in their early 30s, imagine the code that would emerge if you used "convenience" sampling and interviewed doctoral students in the psychology, sociology, and anthropology departments. Your raw information would substantially and dramatically show that people in their early 30s are deeply concerned with learning, producing useful insights (or at least producing insights that are publishable!), and working long hours. These are not the themes that you hear from people of this age on television programs such as *Friends, Ellen, Melrose Place, Thirtysomething,* or *Seinfeld.* It is not that doctoral students are not normal people. But they have a shared preoccupation with entering their profession, testing themselves or passing through the rites of passage to be accepted into their profession, and learning. They are a particular sample with embedded characteristics.

Preventing or lessening the obstacles and confusions of sampling is helped by

1. Reviewing the unit of analysis versus the unit of coding: Who or what am I observing/analyzing? How do I want to encode it?
2. Clarifying the unit of analysis and the unit of coding (Chapter 3 is devoted to these issues)
3. Examining the sampling of units of analysis and units of coding from multiple perspectives and possibly asking a number of colleagues to review and "reality-test" the appropriateness and adequacy of your sampling plan
4. Establishing a protocol or guide for information collection

Of course, when in doubt, increase your sampling of people, events, time, and so forth. There may not be greater insight in greater numbers of units of analysis or coding, but there is an increase in the comfort and confidence that your raw information is not contaminated by unforeseen forces.

Sound research design is imperative for good qualitative research. Unfortunately, novices and lazy researchers often confuse the departure from quantitative methods with departure from logic and thorough research design. Criterion development, criterion sampling, type-of-information sampling, event sampling, unit-of-coding sampling, and unit-of-analysis sampling are only a few of the types of design issues that must be considered before collecting raw information (Mason, 1996).

Mood and Style

Qualitative research *is* subjective. Therefore, many factors may threaten the quality of information collection, processing, and analysis. All of this happens before the possibility of confusion in interpretation. The researcher's fatigue and/or sensory overload, frustration with the raw information or concepts, or confusion as to the unit of analysis and unit of coding will decrease his or her ability to conduct thematic analysis. Ability to sense themes and develop codes, as well as to apply the codes consistently, will be adversely affected by the arousal effect of the source material on the researcher; his or her cognitive style and tendencies toward wanting a clear, definite correct answer will interfere. Tolerance of ambiguity is a precursor to the type of openness discussed earlier as a desired characteristic of the researcher using thematic analysis. Patient perseverance pays off in finding themes amid voluminous qualitative information. Even when you have developed or found an appropriate and usable thematic code and have established interrater reliability (i.e., consistency of judgment), there will be atrophy of skill and loss of accuracy over time and during periods of stress, fatigue, or distraction.

The following will help prevent or lessen errors and distractions related to the researcher's mood and style:

1. Being rested and not preoccupied when conducting thematic analysis
2. Developing or finding a clear code
3. Establishing consistency of judgment among "multiple perceivers"
4. Having the self-control to stop coding if you find yourself preoccupied or worried about something else and to return to the research at a later time when you are in a different state
5. Suspending analytic frameworks and rational judgments to "go with" the raw information—developing the "inner game" of coding

Latent- Versus Manifest-Content Analysis

Nowhere is the challenge of thematic analysis more evident than in the unfolding of meaning from dreams. The science or art of dream analysis is the use of thematic analysis to decipher the latent meaning of dreams (Campbell, 1949; Fromm, 1951; Hobson, 1988; Klinger, 1971; Moss, 1967; Murray, 1959; Stevens, 1995). Manifest-content analysis can be considered the analysis of the visible or apparent content of something. For example, an analysis of the number of times that a person uses the word *excellent* would be an example of manifest-content analysis. We know the degree to which he or she uses the word. We can describe the sentences and phrases in which he or she uses it. We can compare his or her use of the word to that of others in his or her social group, social class, or culture. But to explain or understand the meaning of the word to the person, or the meaning of the word as it was used in a particular sentence or moment, we must turn to latent-content analysis. Latent-content analysis is looking at the underlying aspects of the phenomenon under observation. It is more interpretive than manifest-content analysis. If a researcher is trained in content analysis, typically he or she is trained in one of these approaches. Thematic analysis enables the researcher to use both manifest- and latent-content analysis *at the same time.*

Many forms of content analysis have historically remained at the manifest level, with techniques such as the General Inquirer (Stone, Dunphy, Smith, & Ogilvie, 1966). Increased sophistication in the interpretation of such results and expanded applications have resulted in approaches such as the Content Analysis of Verbal Behavior (CAVE; Gottschalk, 1995) that move beyond the manifest, literal level toward becoming interpretive. Advances in computer hardware and software have helped this type of analysis to become accessible to many researchers.

Dream Analysis: Sensing Themes in Thought

Dream analysis will now be used to explore *sensing themes,* the first step in developing the skills needed for using thematic analysis. The following section can be used as an illustration of the beginning of thematic analysis or as an exercise for those seeking to develop their skills. The examples and exercise will also provide the opportunity to discuss the differences between manifest- and latent-content analysis. For the exercise, we shall examine dreams from two prominent authors: two dreams from Carl Gustav Jung and two dreams from Robert Louis Stevenson. The dreams are from an anthology compiled by Brian Hill (1967), called *Gates of Horn and Ivory.*

To do this exercise, read each of the following four dreams. Identify elements in the dreams that you believe to be important in understanding their meaning. Identify themes or patterns that you see in the dreams from the same author. Consider differences between the dreams and themes of the two authors. Following the dreams, I will offer a rudimentary analysis of the dreams and a brief description of the life of each author.

Selected Dreams of Carl Gustav Jung

The White Bird:

In the dream I found myself in a magnificent Italian loggia with pillars, a marble floor, and a marble balustrade. I was sitting on a gold Renaissance chair; in front of me was a table of rare beauty. It was made of green stone, like emerald. There I sat, looking out into the distance, for the loggia was set high up on the tower of a castle. My children were sitting at the table too.

Suddenly a white bird descended, a small sea-gull or a dove. Gracefully it came to rest on the table, and I signed to the children to be still so that they would not frighten away the pretty white bird. Immediately, the dove is transformed into a little girl, about eight years of age, with golden blonde hair. She ran off with the children and played with them among the colonnades of the castle.

I remained lost in thought, musing about what I had just experienced. The little girl returned and tenderly placed her arms round my neck. Then she suddenly vanished; the dove was back and spoke slowly in a human voice, "Only in the first hours of the night can I transform myself into a human being, while the male dove is busy with the twelve dead." Then she flew off into the blue air, and I awoke. (Jung, 1961, p. 171)

The Magnolia Tree:

I found myself in a dirty, sooty city. It was night, and winter, and dark, and raining. I was in Liverpool. With a number of Swiss—say, half a dozen—I walked through the dark streets. I had the feeling that there we were coming from the harbor, and that the real city was actually up above, on the cliffs. We climbed up there. It reminded me of Basel, where the market is down below and then you go up through the Totengasschen ("Alley of the Dead"), which leads to a plateau above and so to the Petersplatz and the Peterskirche. When we reached the plateau, we found a broad square dimly illuminated by street lights, into which many streets converged. The various quarters of the city were arranged radially round the square. In the center was a round pool, and in the middle of it a small island. While everything round about was obscured by rain, fog, smoke, and dimly lit darkness, the little island blazed with sunlight. On it stood a single tree, a magnolia, in a shower of reddish blossoms. It was as though the tree stood in the sunlight and were at the same time the source of light. My companions commented on the abominable weather, and obviously did not see the tree. They spoke of another Swiss who was living in Liverpool, and expressed surprise that he should have settled here. I was carried away by the beauty of the flowering tree and the sunlit island, and thought, "I know very well why he has settled here." Then I awoke. (Jung, 1961, pp. 197-198)

Selected Dreams of Robert Louis Stevenson

The Yard Dog:

It seemed to him that he was in the first floor of a rough hill-farm. The room showed some poor efforts at gentility, a carpet on the floor, a piano, I think, against the wall; but, for all these refinements, there was no mistaking he was in a moorland place, among hillside people, and set in miles of heather. He looked down from the window upon a bare farmyard, that seemed to have been long disused. A great, uneasy stillness lay upon the world. There was no sign of the farm-folk, or of any livestock, save for an old, brown, curly dog of the retriever breed, who sat close in against the wall of the house and seemed to be dozing. Something about this dog disquieted the dreamer; it was quite a nameless feeling, for the beast looked right enough—indeed, he was so old and dull and dusty and broken-down, that he should rather have awakened pity; and yet the conviction came and grew upon the dreamer that this was no proper dog at all, but something hellish. A great many dozing summer fields hummed about the yard; and presently the dog thrust forth his paw, caught a fly in his open palm, carried it to his mouth like an ape, and looked suddenly up at the dreamer in the window, winked at him with one eye. (Hill, 1967, p. 132)

The Staircase:

Well, in his dream life, he passed a long day in the surgical theater, his heart in his mouth, his teeth on edge, seeing monstrous malformations and the abhorred dexterity of surgeons. In a heavy, rainy, foggy evening he came forth into the South Bridge, turned up the High Street, and entered the door of a tall *land,* at the top of which he supposed himself to lodge. All night long, in his wet clothes, he climbed the stairs, stair after stair in endless series, and at every second flight a flaring lamp with a reflector. All night long, he brushed by single persons passing downward—beggarly women of the street, great, weary, muddy laborers, poor scarecrows of men, pale parodies of women— but all drowsy and weary like himself, and all single, and all brushing against him as they passed. In the end, out of a northern window, he would see day beginning to whiten over the Firth, give up the ascent, turn to descend, and in a breath be back again upon the streets, in his wet clothes, in the wet, haggard dawn, trudging to another day of monstrosities and operations. (Hill, 1967, pp. 131-132)

Themes Sensed or Seen in These Dreams

Before continuing, consider the exercise. As mentioned previously, you are asked to identify elements in the dreams that you believe to be important in understanding their meaning. Identify themes or patterns that you see in the dreams from the same author. Consider differences between the dreams and themes between the two authors.

Whether you have chosen to do the exercise or not, an analysis of the dreams may help to illustrate the importance of manifest and latent analysis and the differences between them. The following themes are from discussion of the dreams in my doctoral seminar, as well as my own analysis of these dreams.

The White Bird: There is a visual elegance in this dream. The dreamer is in the context of his family, specifically his children. There seems to be a tension between loving his children and letting them go. There is a tender embrace. There is the mystery of the transformation of the dove into the little girl and back again.

A Freudian analysis might offer the dream wish as a desire to be loved or to love another who is protected by someone. To extend the analysis further, the tender embrace by the little girl who tells the dreamer that she can only become human when the male dove is busy suggests inhibited desire for a younger woman, if not the confusion of loving one's own children.

For a Jungian analysis, we have the benefit of Jung's comments on his own dream (Jung, 1961, pp. 171-174). He had the dream around Christmas in 1912. His personal context included his growing separation from Freud and the general disorientation that this was causing him. He described the turmoil of trying to find his own approach to the human psyche, dream analysis, and such. Could it be that Freud is like the male dove? Only when the male dove is busy, with his attention diverted, can the young girl become human. Could Jung have been describing a prerequisite for his becoming human—that is, becoming his own person with his own theories?

In reacting to the dream, Jung was struck with the emerald table and the similarity to the story of the Tabula Smaragdina from the legend of Hermes Trismegistos. On the table were engraved the tenets of alchemical wisdom. Jung's own fascination with alchemy and transformation are relevant. He went on, in describing his reactions and thoughts about the dream, to say that he kept considering various meanings of the twelve dead. He considered the 12 apostles, 12 signs of the zodiac, and 12 months of the year, but nothing emerged as meaningful. "I could find no solution to the enigma. Finally I had to give it up. All I knew with any certainty was that the dream indicated an unusual activation of the unconscious" (Jung, 1961, p. 172). He also discussed how this was the period of his life in which his theories were beginning to form—theories that seemed to require his break with Freud to develop. Let us consider the cultural context. The world was on the brink of war. Revolution was stirring in Russia. Switzerland, unlike Vienna, was somewhat removed from the turmoil. The dream, in Jungian terms, seems to express the dreamer's (in this case, Jung's own) sense of impending transformation and a new beginning predicated on the distraction of a force that inhibited his transformation.

The Magnolia Tree: The dramatic red tree in the sunlight is like fire and the "burning bush" image from the Old Testament of the Bible. This may represent God. The dreamer sees God, while the heathens about him do not. He sees truth; the others do not. They are "fogged" or "clouded" in their vision. A Freudian analysis might offer the "dream wish" of overcoming death and possibly even being godlike. The divergence of the dreamer's perception from that of the "others" may reflect the dreamer's disdain for the insensitive people who surround him.

Again, we have the benefit of Jung's own comments, starting with his statement that he had the dream in 1928. He had been developing his theories and publishing. Jung had concluded that the goal of psychic development was the development of the self. An inner peace had returned, he reported, as he began to feel that he had achieved the key insights for which he was searching. At the time of the dream, he had been painting a picture of a golden, well-fortified castle. On reflecting why the picture seemed oddly Chinese looking, he remembered that at the time of the painting, Richard Wilhelm of Frankfort had sent him a thousand-year-old Chinese text about the "yellow castle, the germ of the immortal body" (Jung, 1961, p. 197). He stated,

> This dream represented my situation at the time. . . . Everything was extremely unpleasant, black and opaque—just as I felt then. But I had had a vision of unearthly beauty, and that was why I was able to live at all. Liverpool is the "pool of life." The "liver," according to an old view, is the seat of life—that which "makes to live." (p. 198)

He continued,

> This dream brought with it a sense of finality. I saw that here the goal had been revealed. One could not go beyond the center. The center is the goal and everything is directed toward that center. Through this dream I understood that the self is the principle and archetype of orientation and meaning. (pp. 198-199)

If I can be sufficiently arrogant to embellish on Jung's analysis of his own dream, it also seems that he felt a spiritual enlightenment associated with his insight into the human psyche and felt that others did not understand it or that they had not recognized the greatness of his contribution yet!

The Yard Dog: There is uneasiness, trickery, and deceit in this dream. The dreamer experiences shame at some part of himself. He is presented with evil disguised as something lovable and comfortable—that is, the dog. A Jungian analysis might offer the central theme as the expressed desire for movement, or for transformation from good to evil and back again. There is a mystery of veiled power and playfulness as well. A Freudian analysis might say that the dream wish was the desire to be exposed—that is, to have the unexpected part of himself (i.e., unexpected by others) which is playful, shown to the world.

The Staircase: This dream is filled with disturbing sensations of uneasiness, fatigue, and boredom. The reader feels as if he or she is also cold, wet, and deeply tired. The dichotomies (i.e., day and night, up and down, men and women, a surgeon engaged in monstrosities, people seemingly alone but brushing up against each other) suggest a conflict between opposing forces, reinforced by the allusion to a class distinction. A Jungian analysis might offer the central theme as one of feeling lost and desiring direction. A Freudian analysis might say that the dream wish was a desire to alleviate the boredom, to not end up like the rest, and to be different.

The themes may be more or less explicit and clear in your analysis. The interpretations of the central theme or dream wish are offered as *possible* Jungian and Freudian interpretations and are not meant to be the "correct" answers. They may not be the analysis that Carl Jung or Sigmund Freud or a psychotherapist today might offer. In the case of Jung's dreams, we have the benefit, or the distraction, of his own comments on the dreams. The exercise with the dreams is meant to stimulate and provoke your initial exploration of thematic analysis through "sensing themes" in the dreams.

Most readers have probably felt a compelling difference between these two sets of dreams. Some readers will have identified simple, descriptive characteristics of each that point up the differences between the two sets: for example, that Jung's dreams seem hopeful and Stevenson's seem full of despair, or that Jung's dreams are full of light and airiness, whereas Stevenson's are full of darkness and dankness. Some readers will have identified more elaborate thematic differences, with literary or artistic metaphors—for example, that Jung's dreams are like a Tintoretto or Renoir painting, whereas Stevenson's dreams are like an Escher or Bosch print.

Analysis of these two sets of dreams might result in the following list of comparative themes:

Jung's Dreams	Stevenson's Dreams
Hopeful	Despairing, fatalistic
Magical	Mysterious
Jekyll	Hyde
Aesthetically pleasing	Dramatic
Light	Dark
Transformative	Tortured and tired
Tintoretto	Escher/Bosch
With others	Alone
Heroic	Demonic
Aristotelian	Platonic
Life after death	Life on earth

Some of these themes are at the manifest level in that they describe the apparent occurrences within the dreams. Describing Jung's dreams as "having a light and airy quality" versus Stevenson's as "dark" would be making an observation about the manifest level of the dreams. You are being descriptive. For the latent level of themes, you must interpret what is meant by something in the dreams. For example, you might say that Jung's dream's show "life after death, or heaven, as a light and pleasing setting" and that Stevenson's dreams show "life on earth to be mysterious and treacherous." You have now taken themes observed in the two sets of dreams and built interpretations about each dreamer's vision of heaven and earth! This has moved to the latent level of thematic analysis.

Once you have identified a variety of themes in these sets of dreams, the question arises, "So what? What do these themes tell us?" One answer, though perhaps simplistic, may be found in the following brief description of the lives of these two authors. You may see clearly the associations between their lives and the themes brought out by the dream analysis, or they may seem like a stretch of the imagination.

Carl Gustav Jung was born in 1875 in Switzerland and died in 1961 in Zurich. His childhood in rural Switzerland was lonely. He was the son of a pastor, who was a kind father. Jung became a physician. He worked at Bleuler's Institute, where he met and became an associate of Freud's between 1907 and 1912. As a personality theorist, psychotherapist, and social theorist, he developed theories of psychological types, integrated religious symbolism into unconscious life, and created the concept of a collective consciousness. Jung is credited with developing the hermetic tradition of analysis, a heretical movement that provided a symbolic map of the consciousness outside of formal religion (e.g., not within the realm of Christianity). He extended his explorations of the human spirit into alchemy, art, and mythology. His best known books include *Psychological Types* (1921), *The Psychology of the Unconscious* (1917), *Symbols of Transformation* (1912), *Psychology and Religion* (1938), and *The Undiscovered Self* (1957).

His fascination with transformation and the spiritual realm was part of his entire life, from his father's preaching to his work on human spirituality. Although he had many different settings for his work, he kept returning to and spent most of his later years in his house on the lake. It was peaceful, somewhat isolated, and a "retreat" for someone considered to be an introvert. The transcendent tone of his dreams and the images they evoked provide a commonality with the overall "color" of his life. He may have had enemies, but the overriding impression in the existing literature and the scholars who cite his intellectual influence on them is a pleasant, revered image. This is in contrast with the tumultuous and perpetual conflict surrounding Freud and his associates and those who, to this day, are expanding, refuting, or critiquing his theories and methods. Jung's continual preoccupation with and exploration of magic, alchemy, and the mystery of the collective human spirit also seem to have parallels in the themes and images in the dreams.

Robert Louis Stevenson was born in 1850 in Edinburgh and died in 1894 in Samoa. He had poor health as a child. Stevenson was the son of a civil engineer. His father was demanding, and the two of them had a painful relationship. Stevenson compromised with his father's insistent wishes for him to study engineering by studying law. In his early adulthood, he met and had a complex relationship with an older woman and her fiancée. He again had a severe illness—this time, tuberculosis. He left for southern France and later would travel frequently to other countries as well. Stevenson began writing at an early age. Later, he came to the United States penniless and ill and was married. After several more illnesses, he continued his travels to Switzerland, to England, back to the United States, and to Samoa. Stevenson received popular acclaim during his lifetime, especially in his later years. Besides writing novels, he also wrote poetry and numerous essays. Some of his best known books are *Treasure Island* (1881), *Kidnapped* (1886), *The Strange Case of Dr. Jekyll and Mr. Hyde* (1886), *The Master of Ballantrae* (1889), and *The Black Arrow* (1888).

Stevenson's life was filled with dramatic ups and downs—like the staircase! His intimate relationships seemed tortured, as his body was with various illnesses. His restlessness was evident in his geographic moves and lack of settling in one cultural setting. The images from his dreams of dark, mysterious settings with hidden evil and monstrous power seem to be a reflection of major elements in his life of struggle, illness, suffering, and conflict with others and social expectations. Even his writing, especially the major pieces of fiction, were about adventure—but always revolving around treachery, betrayal, and the "dark side" of the human psyche.

The intent of this exercise was to illustrate the early stage of thematic analysis, that of sensing themes. This illustration does not offer a complete description of the thematic analysis, but it is an appropriate introduction to using thematic analysis. The attempt to link these authors' dreams to their lives is really a professor's gesture at some interesting connections. The linkages cannot be considered adequate qualitative research into their lives because I have committed three major methodological flaws: (a) potential errors in sampling of their dreams; (b) a simplistic thematic analysis of the dreams; and (c) a cursory review of their lives. The dreams were extracted from Brian Hill's compilation of 300 dreams of notable personalities in history. To be methodologically sound, I would have to investigate his method of sampling: Why these dreams? How accurately were the dreams recorded? When they were previously published, and what was the context and purpose of their publication? But as I have said, my intent was to offer an exercise and illustration, not to conduct life history research on Carl Jung or Robert Louis Stevenson. Conducting the complete process of thematic analysis (as described in Chapter 2), with attention to design and sampling issues (as explained in Chapter 3), could have made this exercise into sound research! But before we explore further the process of thematic analysis, there is a further conceptual benefit that we can derive from dream analysis.

What Is Dream Analysis?

Dreams are dramatic events that do not follow the laws of logic. As mentioned earlier, content analysis can be conducted at the manifest or the latent level. The manifest level of dream analysis would examine the logic inherent in the sequence of the explicit events of the dreams. The latent level of analysis would ask, "What does it mean?"

Dreams have meant many things to people over the history of civilization since the earliest evidence of recorded dreams in the seventh century B.C. and possibly back as far as 3000 B.C. (Stevens, 1995), with evidence from the Egyptians and ancient Greeks, the Indians (in the *Vedas*), and the ancient Chinese. Among the Ashanti, dreams were historically seen as acts to punish a person. Homer portrayed dreams, whether Agamemnon's or Odysseus's premonitions, as visions. In the Bible, dreams appear as visions or as visitations of God or the Holy Ghost. In the Middle Ages in Europe, dreams were viewed as evidence of the presence of the devil and evil spirits. Historically, theories of dreams have fallen into one of three categories (Stevens, 1995): (a) prophecy inspired by supernatural beings, such as gods or devils; (b) experiences of the soul in which the spirit of the person has departed from the body during sleep; or (c) normal mental activity. Current work on dream analysis has continued, with many clinicians and personality theorists developing variations on methods of dream analysis and interpretation, even extending to fascinating and extensive research on the neurophysiology of dreams and dreaming (Hobson, 1988; Stevens, 1995).

Although the assertion is controversial, it can be said that Sigmund Freud's greatest contribution to social science was the development of his theory of dreams and methods of dream analysis (Freud, 1900/1965). It unlocked an arena of human activity for systematic investigation. Freud contended that a dream is a rational production, the result of wishes or desires that have a censor blocking them from consciousness. A dream is composed of repressed ideas and feelings. A parapraxis (i.e., Freudian slip) is a form of conscious-unconscious communication. Therefore, free association is a key method for unlocking the message within a person's dreams.

Freud's approach to dreams and dream analysis is centered on the contention that a "dream wish" is expressed in each dream. This is a wish, rooted in our childhood and/or irrational or forbidden, for which dreams offer hallucinatory fulfillment (Fromm, 1951). The purpose of dream language is to disguise the real affect and message of the dream. A dream is a secret code to be deciphered. Freud described symbols that his thematic analysis had shown to occur frequently in the dreams of his patients. For example, he asserted that trees in a dream may be genital symbols, dancing may be symbolic of sexual pleasure, a journey may be a symbol for death, and any authority figure in the dream may be a symbol for the dreamer's parents.

Freud's theory stated that "dream work" converts the latent "dream wish" into manifest occurrences through symbolic representation and that the analysis of the dream must reverse this conversion. The ego defends itself against awareness of the "real" message of the dream through a number of *ego defense mechanisms.* Four such mechanisms are condensation, displacement, elaboration, and reaction formation; there are others, but these are sufficient for our analysis of the examples. With *condensation,* a dream is made shorter than real time, leaves things out and combines images for efficiency (e.g., the dreamer's feelings toward his or her father and an important teacher may be combined into a dreamed encounter with an authority figure of different form). With *displacement,* an important element appears as unimportant. With *elaboration,* gaps in manifest content of the dream (i.e., the story of the dream) are filled in so that the story appears to make sense. With *reaction formation,* elements in the dream may represent the opposite of what they seem.

Carl Jung's approach to dream analysis went in another direction (Abell, 1957; Jung, 1961, 1964). The purpose of a dream was to enhance individuation—the development of the person. Dreams had a structure similar to fiction or specifically Greek tragedy, starting with the "exposition" setting the time and place, "the development of the plot," the culmination, and the conclusion (Stevens, 1995). Dream interpretation required the dreamer's amplification of the personal meaning of the dream or its elements. As Stevens (1995) explained and described in detail, dream analysis from Jung's perspective followed an understanding of the dreamer's personal context, cultural context, and archetypal context.

Jung contended that dreams are an expression of the wisdom of the unconscious. Because the unconscious is capable of assuming intelligence and purposiveness that are superior to conscious insight, Jung thought that dreams may reflect a person's enlightened thought. He considered spirituality an integral aspect of personality and saw dreams as a possible form of religious expression.

> Jung's dream theory emphasizes transparency and creativity, in contrast to Freud's emphasis on obscurity and psychopathology. While Freud admitted that some dreams do not display disguise and censorship, he thought that the most unique dream features reflect the operation of these concealing processes. Jung saw dreams as no less symbolic but viewed the symbols as more directly expressive of universal human concerns and as not necessarily serving the purpose of disguise. (Hobson, 1988, p. 65)

According to Jung's theory of the development of the collective unconscious, dreams could transcend the individual. The collective unconscious is the storehouse of latent memory traces inherited from our cultural and ancestral past. Jung believed that analysis of a dream series was important.

Images from the collective unconscious appearing in an individual's personality appeared to coalesce into a set of patterns that Jung called *archetypes.* Identification of these archetypes resulted from Jung's use of thematic analysis! Each archetype is a motif that Jung considered a universal thought or idea containing a large amount of emotion. Personal complexes or personality disorders usually reflect one of these universal types.

Freud and Jung were not the only developers of approaches to dream analysis. Other approaches to dream analysis include kinetic and Gestalt dream analysis and have been set forth by a wide range of noted authors, such as Alfred Adler, Erich Fromm, Calvin Hall, James Hillman, and Fritz Perls.

Manifest and Latent Levels of Thematic Analysis

Dream analysis provides a relatively easy example of "sensing themes." The type of dream analysis that both Freud and Jung developed and used was a latent-level thematic analysis. They were asking what was meant by the dream elements and the dream as a whole. They were "interpreting" the dream as told or recalled by the dreamer. They not only observed themes within the individual's dream but proceeded to identify patterns or themes across his or her dreams. They even took thematic analysis to another level and developed methods of analyzing dreams across groups of people.

With other types of source material, or with raw information in qualitative studies, both the manifest and latent levels of analysis will probably yield insights. The researcher must be cautious. The manifest level of analysis is a seductively easy way to get some observations (e.g., counting the number of superlatives in a person's essay to assess the degree of passion in the person's writing). It is also a way to feel a sense of "control" over the material or raw information when latent themes are elusive. Unfortunately, this easy way out leaves much of the richness of the raw information unanalyzed. Similarly, the latent level of analysis can easily get so complicated and intricate that you forget the meaning of the themes and why you were exploring this unit of analysis.

CHAPTER TWO

Developing Themes and Codes

The use of thematic analysis involves three distinct stages: Stage I, deciding on sampling and design issues; Stage II, developing themes and a code; and Stage III, validating and using the code. Within the second stage, there are three different ways to develop a thematic code: (a) theory driven, (b) prior data or prior research driven, and (c) inductive (i.e., from the raw data) or data driven.

These approaches can be considered to form a continuum from theory-driven to data-driven approaches. Each has benefits and challenges for the researcher. The continuum can be said to reflect increasing uncertainty and ambiguity of the analysis and code, and consequently increasing discomfort of the researcher, as well as increasing time to develop the code. Thus, for example, a theory-driven approach is comfortable for many researchers because they are starting from their own theory or someone else's and then proceeding to develop their thematic code consistent with their theory.

All of these approaches to developing themes and a code move the researcher toward theory development. They differ, however, in the degree to which the thematic analysis starts with a theory or the raw information. When entering the path of the data-driven approach, researchers must have a great deal of faith that they will arrive at a desirable destination, especially because they do not know where it will be, what it will look like once they are there, and how long it will take.

The continuum typically reflects the decreasing likelihood of achieving high interrater reliability, or consistency of judgment. In research studies of multiple units of analysis (such as a number of people, couples, cultures, or organizations) and comparative studies, the continuum typically reflects decreasing likelihood of achieving validity with the code. In studies of one person, culture, or organization, or with no conceivable comparison, the continuum does *not* imply any relationship to validity of the code.

Data-driven codes are constructed inductively from the raw information. They appear with the words and syntax of the raw information. It is the task of the researcher to interpret the meaning after obtaining the findings and to construct a theory after the discovery of results.

The closeness of the code to the raw information increases the likelihood that various people examining the raw information will perceive and therefore encode the information similarly. The result is a higher interrater reliability. Because a data-driven code is highly sensitive to the context of the raw information, one is more likely to obtain validity against criteria and construct variables. This increases with the use of the data-driven approach more than with the theory-driven approach.

Working directly from the raw information enhances appreciation of the information, in addition to eliminating intermediaries as potentially contaminating factors. With a complete view of the information available, the researcher can appreciate gross (i.e., easily evident) and intricate (i.e., difficult-to-discern) aspects of the information. Previously silenced voices or perspectives inherent in the information can be brought forward and recognized.

The approach of developing a code on the basis of prior research places the researcher approximately in the middle of the continuum. If several studies are used as the basis for the code, the researcher is near the middle of the continuum. As the number of studies and specifically studies using the same type of raw information (e.g., samples of thought from the same projective test, samples of interaction from the same type of social setting) increases, the researcher moves toward the data-driven end of the continuum.

The two ends of the continuum can also be examined in terms of discovery-oriented research. Diesing (1971) contended that deductive approaches to discovery are based on an assumption that there are "laws" or principles that can be applied to the phenomenon. Insight can be derived from application of the model to a set of information, whether through hypothesis testing or through searching for consistencies and anomalies. On the other hand, an inductive approach searching for patterns is based on the "facts," or information being studied. Diesing (1971) claimed that it is not possible to "deduce an unknown part of a pattern from a known part" (pp. 163-164). Of course, he added that a pattern model approach—what I am calling inductive—is "rarely if ever finished completely" (p. 164) and that the concepts or models being discovered and built are subject to change during the process of inquiry.

Any of these three approaches can be used with any of the different types of raw information. Each of these approaches can be used with studies of a case of one; studies of similarities among individuals, groups, organizations, or cultures; or comparative analyses of multiple people, groups, organizations, and cultures that differ on some explicit criterion. Regardless of the approach to identification of themes and code development, certain characteristics of a code have proven useful to researchers. When these are present, the code is more likely to yield meaningful results.

Structure of a Useful, Meaningful Code

A good thematic code is one that captures the qualitative richness of the phenomenon. It is usable in the analysis, interpretation, and presentation of the research. From the perspective of scoring and scaling for quantitative analysis, a good code will also have the maximum probability of producing high interrater reliability and validity. A good thematic code should have five elements:

1. A label (i.e., a name)
2. A definition of what the theme concerns (i.e., the characteristic or issue constituting the theme)
3. A description of how to know when the theme occurs (i.e., indicators on how to "flag" the theme)
4. A description of any qualifications or exclusions to the identification of the theme
5. Examples, both positive and negative, to eliminate possible confusion when looking for the theme

The label should be developed last in the process of writing or creating the code. To be of most utility, the label should be (a) conceptually meaningful to the phenomenon being studied; (b) clear and concise, communicating the essence of the theme in the fewest words possible; and (c) close to the data. The more the label requires a conceptual step or leap from the raw information, the more interpretation has crept into the code development process. The desire is to minimize the interpretation at this point in the process and save it for the analysis following code development, during the code application stages of the research. Unfortunately, a complex name or label provokes thoughts that creep into this stage. A conceptual leap reflected in a label that interprets the theme may lead to misinterpretation or alterations by other researchers when they are applying the code to new raw information.

An example occurred a number of years ago when I and my colleagues were engaged in a review of managerial and leadership competency research conducted by David G. Winter for the U.S. Navy (Winter, 1979). In the original competency studies conducted from 1975 through 1977, a cognitive characteristic called "conceptual ability" was found to statistically and significantly differentiate superior-performing naval officers and senior enlisted personnel from their less effective counterparts. The ability is also called *pattern recognition* and is defined as the ability to perceive patterns of themes in seemingly random or previously unorganized information. This is the ability that is at the heart of conducting thematic analysis. Professionals who seem to be "natural" at thematic analysis appear to have and use this capability extensively.

After the validation and cross-validation studies, teams of consultants and Navy human resource personnel designed training programs to assist in the development of management and leadership. The training courses developed modules addressing each of the competencies found to significantly differentiate superior naval officers and senior enlisted personnel. The module devoted to addressing this particular competency (i.e., conceptual ability) used techniques of rational problem solving. It led participants through a process of rationally reducing a situation into various components or causal factors, using techniques such as force-field and situation analysis, then determining the causal factors that had the most impact, and finally determining desirable ways to overcome or eliminate these causal factors.

The observation made during the review meetings was that these activities seemed to address a cognitive ability, but one quite different from the "sensing and intuitive" talent that we were calling conceptual ability. The activities were training people in deductive thinking processes, when in fact the competency was one of inductive thinking. Interviews with members of the original training design team revealed that they had decided that the label *conceptual ability* was too abstract and unclear for the trainers and participants in the courses. In searching through the options, they had observed that the competency was used in solving problems, so they had relabeled it *problem solving*. Once that new label appeared, the earlier exercises in the module, including brainstorming and other inductive techniques such as frame- or set-breaking exercises, were dropped and replaced with deductive, rational approaches to problem identification and problem solving. The subsequent trainers and people involved in redesign following initial pilot courses felt that these types of exercises were better methods to develop "problem-solving" ability. The label had replaced the definition and code as the determining characteristics of the competency. The researcher can unintentionally hasten this process of confusion, obfuscation, and distortion by using labels that, instead of sticking close to the raw information and its own language, form, and style, reflect what the researcher wants the theme to be (i.e., his or her own values or theory).

Developing a Theory-Driven Code

Theory-driven code development is probably the most frequently used approach in social science research. The researcher begins with his or her theory of what occurs and then formulates the signals, or indicators, of evidence that would support this theory. The elements of the code are derived from the hypotheses or elements of the theory.

The anticipated "meaning" of the expected results of the analysis determines the composition of the code. The wording of the themes emerges from the theorist's construction of the meaning and style of communication or expression of the elements of the theory. The code is therefore often in the language of the researcher's field, filled with the special meanings and jargon. The value of this type of code is highly dependent on the theoretical sensitivity of the researcher (Strauss & Corbin, 1990). The degree of conceptual rigidity shown by the researcher increases the likelihood of a code that is difficult to use and has low validity and for which it is difficult to establish sufficient interrater reliability. One variant of the theory-driven approach is Miller and Crabtree's (1992) "template analytic technique," in which the researcher uses someone else's code or framework to process and/or analyze the information.

The preference for theory-driven codes is not surprising, given the professional standards, practices, and socialization into the various disciplines. Socialization within each field begins at admission to graduate school and continues at a feverish pace until the award of tenure if someone is academically bound. Within the social sciences and humanities, disciplines differ as to their "preference" regarding the acceptability of thematic analysis as a research process and the appropriate basis for development of thematic codes. For example, clinical psychology and cultural anthropology have typically favored inductively derived (i.e., data-driven) codes. This is in contrast to their sister fields of social psychology, experimental psychology, and some areas of comparative anthropology, in which theory-driven codes have prevailed as "appropriate" approaches.

There are probably many reasons that such preferences have become established, from dominant learning styles of researchers in a field to the degree of sophistication and length of detailed study in a field. Differences in the epistemologies of these disciplines are probably also the sources for such preferences. Learning and cognitive style differences of various fields explain some of the variation. For example, people in clinical psychology tend to have learning styles, as measured through the Learning Style Inventory (Kolb, 1984), that can be described as "divergent." This learning style involves a preference for concrete experiences and reflection on them, resulting in the use of inductive thought processes. The preference of people in clinical psychology for dealing with areas of human behavior and experience that are "fuzzier" and appear less definable may contribute to the appropriateness of the divergent learning style to phenomena of interest.

People in philosophy tend to have learning styles described as "assimilative," suggesting a tendency toward basing learning on a theory (i.e., abstract concepts) and then proceeding to interpret phenomena. A theory-driven approach to code development would appear more natural to people in philosophy.

Observations about the acceptability of thematic analysis and preferred approach to code development can be made through examination of the academic, professional gatekeepers of the fields. What will the journals in the field publish? What methods are taught by the faculty in research methods courses in the doctoral programs?

Given socialization and pressure to complete studies that will be acceptable to journal editors, the convenience and comfort of theory-driven codes create a momentum toward their use. After all, in using a theory-driven code, the researcher is seeking to prove his or her worldview. On the positive side, the goal of all research is to obtain insights and to create frameworks with which to understand the world around us. These frameworks, when fully developed, are theories. If theory is the eventual goal of research, it is natural for the researcher to have burgeoning theories in his or her mind even at the onset of a research study. Many types of research require it. But within qualitative research, the researcher may be exploring something not previously understood or even examined. In these situations, a theory-driven approach comes with the problems being discussed here.

Despite the pressure toward its use, the theory-driven approach involves difficulties, often resulting in lower interrater reliability (i.e., lower consistency of judgments) and lower validity. Some of these factors were mentioned earlier in this chapter. Theory-driven codes are relatively more sensitive to projection on the part of the researcher and to the impact of his or her cultural bias. If I am generating the themes and wording of the code from my theory, my beliefs and assumptions will be the basis for the code. It will be difficult to discover what "the data may be saying."

In addition, theory-driven codes are developed "out of context" of the type of material to be coded. Therefore, the specifics of the operational code (i.e., the detailed code to be used on the source material) may be inappropriate to the material to be coded. This goes against the recommendations of Wolcott (1994) to stay as close to the data as possible and Strauss and Corbin's (1990) concept of "open coding," or naming and categorizing phenomena by "close examination of the data."

For example, suppose that a code to assess thought processes is developed from a theory. This code may include themes describing the details of a person's thought process (i.e., step-by-step description of how a problem is mentally approached). If the raw information being coded is verbal interactions of a husband and wife at the dinner table, or a sales team making a call on an important client, it is unlikely that the individuals will openly discuss their actual thought processes. They may describe conclusions, take positions, or anticipate the other person's positions and make statements related to the "negotiation" aspect of the interaction rather than their thought processes. In this case, a theory-driven code will not be useful without further development. Results from its use without further development will be of limited value.

Stage I: Sampling and Design Issues

With the theory-driven approach, the sampling and design issues must be geared to the theory. The number of units of analysis appropriate or sufficient and aspects of the potential stratification of the sample desired (Chapter 3 will discuss this in more detail) must be consistent with the theory.

Stage II: Developing Themes and a Code

There are three steps in developing themes and a code from a theory-driven approach: (a) generating a code, (b) reviewing and revising the code in the context of the nature of the raw information, and (c) determining the reliability of the coders and therefore the code. In the first step, the themes are generated from reading and contemplating the theory, prior-research findings, and/or the codes used in previous research. Because most graduate courses and training involve development of this skill and training in this process, it will not be elaborated here. The desired structure of a code is described in detail later in this chapter.

The second step involves reviewing and possibly rewriting the themes and code emerging from the first step. Because theory and previous research are driving the creation or adoption of the themes, it is essential to check their compatibility with the raw information of your current study. Are the themes using words, syntax, and format that will be understandable to whoever is trying to find the themes in the raw information? This step is like taking a framework written in German and trying to use it to identify themes in Japanese haiku (poetry). You could not do it without translating both the framework and the poetry into the same language. If you put both into a language other than Japanese, you will lose the nuances and intricacies of the haiku, which is known for its exceedingly terse but rich use of language, image, rhythm, and symbols. Meanwhile, the German language is known for its detail in communicating specific meaning and not its terseness. To carry the analogy a little further, to have a useful framework for analysis, you would have to translate both into the same language and then rewrite the framework to be appropriate to the style and syntax of the poetry. The same is true with theory-driven themes and codes. You must determine the applicability of the code to the raw information.

The third step is determining the reliability of the coders and the code. This will be discussed at length in Chapter 7.

Stage III: Validating and Using the Code

The researcher began the inquiry to generate understanding, obtain insights, or build on the work of others. The first two stages in using thematic analysis are for the purpose of using the themes and code in Stage III to validate the code and then interpret its meaning. With theory-driven code development, this is the easiest stage. The researcher started with the theory, so once the observations are made about the presence or absence (or degree of presence or absence) of the themes in the raw information, the interpretation is a direct commentary on the theory. The theory or parts of it are either confirmed or refuted. Of course, often the results require modifying the theory.

Prior-Research-Driven Code Development

A review of the literature, typical of the research process, provides insight into the possible development of a thematic code. Codes used by other researchers and their findings provide the most direct help in developing a code from prior data or prior research. Sometimes the series of findings and refuted hypotheses also provides elements helpful in constructing a code. This approach is similar to Miller and Crabtree's (1992) "editing style of analysis" and lends itself to what Strauss and Corbin (1990) called "axial coding" in clustering or reconfiguring categories identified or developed by others.

Using someone else's code requires development of interrater reliability; in this situation, it would be classified as rater-to-expert reliability, as discussed in Chapter 7. With this approach, the researcher is building on prior research that has established valid codes. Because of their established validity, the codes probably take into account the "context" of the raw information in their wording and syntax. As long as the current researcher is using the codes with the same or similar raw information, the problem discussed for the theory-driven approach is obviated. But if thematic codes were constructed and validated on autobiographical essays and the current researcher wants to use them with videotaped family interactions, the wording and syntax of the codes may not be directly applicable.

Unfortunately, the use of prior data and research as the basis for development of a code means that the researcher accepts another researcher's assumptions, projections, and biases. The appropriateness of the detail in the code to the nature of the source material on which it will be used creates the same difficulties as discussed for theory-driven code development. Nonetheless, as shown in the next example from alcohol and aggression research, building on earlier research can be an effective technique for the researcher to contribute to the development of knowledge and not always feel as if he or she has to "invent the wheel" each time he or she wants to go somewhere! The steps in code development using a prior-research-driven approach are the same steps as outlined in the previous section on theory-driven code development.

An Example Using Theory-Driven
and Prior-Research-Driven Codes

An example of a study in which two codes were developed, one from theory and one from prior research, occurred in the studies of the effect of alcohol consumption on aggressive behavior of men that I conducted in the early 1970s (Boyatzis, 1973, 1974, 1975, 1983). The intent of the studies was to assess the direct impact of drinking alcoholic beverages on aggressive behavior of men.

Stage I: Sampling and Design Issues

The aggressive behavior was observed and videotaped in a typical social setting in which men drank. Volunteers were recruited through local newspapers in the Cambridge, Watertown, and Somerville areas of Massachusetts. They were screened to eliminate people currently under treatment for health problems and to eliminate people with current or a history of alcohol-related problems or abuse. The 157 men participating in the experimental sessions ranged in age from 25 to 50 years old (average age was 32) and had varied occupations; the group included laborers, skilled craftsmen, public service employees, nonmanagerial office workers, managers, and some professionals. Forty-seven percent were currently married, and 38% had completed college. The men completed a battery of psychological tests and attended an evening "get-together" in a simulated neighborhood bar atmosphere. They were video-taped at fixed intervals early, middle, and late in the evening. Breathalyzers were used early, middle, and late in the evening to determine blood alcohol concentration. At some of the sessions, only distilled spirits were drunk, at others, only beer; and at others, only juices and soft drinks.

The videotaping was done by focusing on each participant for 30 seconds for five complete rounds of tape early, middle, and late in each session. In addition, 10 minutes of general group shots were taken early in the evening, and 20 minutes of general group shots were taken in the middle and late evening periods. The timing of each taping period was preset according to the starting time of the evening get-together. Each session was "led" by a male compatriot of mine who was part of the research team or myself. One person worked the video camera for all sessions.

Each participant was coded for the presence or absence of each of the 11 aggressive behavior codes and the six social behavior codes during each of his 30-second filmed periods. Also during the periods in which the general group was filmed, a person could be coded for any one of the codes' being present or absent during an interaction. An event, episode, or interaction during the periods in which the general group was filmed was defined as "a period of interaction between two or more people in which the flow of communication is in one direction concerning the same issue. In other words, a conversation may be a series of events that are scorable." Each participant's frequency of each of the behaviors was summed for the early, middle, and late periods to generate an aggressive behavior score and a social behavior score (Boyatzis, 1973, p.34).

Stage II: Developing Themes and a Code (Steps 1 and 2)

The thematic code for aggressive behavior was built on earlier extensive behavioral and psychological research from Bales' (1970) interaction process analysis code, the work of McClelland, Davis, Kalin, and Wanner (1972), and my own earlier work on alcoholism rehabilitation techniques (Boyatzis, 1976; Cutter, Boyatzis, & Clancy, 1977). In each of these earlier studies, codes of behavior had been developed and used. Aspects of the various codes relating to aggressive behavior were studied and integrated into one code. For illustration, 5 of the 11 themes coded for aggressive behavior were

> "Joking: poking fun at someone present or an absent person or group (e.g., telling ethnic jokes); telling a story or humorous anecdote intended to belittle someone or a group, or make them look foolish" (p. 31).
>
> "Dramatizes: caricaturing or mimicking someone to expose their foolishness or embarrass them; showing disgust or horror" (p. 31).
>
> "Challenging: asking or demanding relevance of task, or instructions; questioning competence of authority or his right to be an authority (his legitimacy); throwing 'the finger'; smiling at the camera" (p. 32).
>
> "Controlling: attempts to control, direct, or supervise the actions of another, others (like telling someone to do something) which are not 'challenging'; actions such as pointing, pushing, or statements which are commands" (p. 32).
>
> "Baiting: teasing, taunting, heckling, scoffing, or actions intended to antagonize another (like shouting a zero score in a dart game, or shouting along with each throw)" (p. 32).

The thematic code for social behavior was developed from theory. Members of the research team and colleagues asked what possible forms of social or prosocial behavior might be demonstrated in this type of drinking context. We used theories of what constitutes prosocial behavior and altruism. For illustration, three of the six themes developed and used for the social behavior code were (Boyatzis, 1973)

> "Greeting another person: waving, drawing near, saying hello, introducing self, shaking hands" (p. 33).
>
> "Solidarity: sign of being with another in a 'group' (alliance) effort or cause, like doing something (cooperative) together, backing another's actions or statements, publicly announcing joint membership in coalition or group (like being members of same club or union), smiling with group humor" (p. 33).
>
> "Succorance: accepting help from another, thanking someone, giving them esteem for an act done on behalf of person doing the thanking" (p. 33).

Stage II: Developing Themes and a Code (Step 3)

The coding was done by two males, each trained in the two codes. An interrater reliability of $r = .949$ was achieved on the aggressive behavior code, and an interrater reliability of $r = .925$ was achieved on the social behavior code.

Stage III: Validating and Using the Code

Highly significant statistical relationships were found between the coded aggressive behavior and amount of alcohol consumed, as well as among the various tests and measures of personality characteristics and aggressive behavior. The social behavior code showed statistically significant results, but they were few, meager by comparison, and more difficult to interpret in light of the wide range of psychological and behavioral data collected. Although this led to clear statements about the effect of alcohol consumption on aggressive behavior, it did not lead to clear statements about the effect on social behavior.

One of the reasons, concluded several years later when these results were compared to those from other studies and those of colleagues, was that the social behavior code was theoretically developed, whereas the aggressive behavior code was adapted from an abundant research literature attempting to measure aggressive behavior. The theory-driven code made sense to those of us on the research team. Because we had been readers of the literature on prosocial behavior and a researcher of affiliation motivation, it could also be said that we were using prior research to formulate our themes and codes. But the research had not examined behavior as much as attitudes, values, and motives (i.e., thought patterns assessed in projective tests). The consequence was that concepts of social behavior were the predominant source of ideas for the social behavior code. Meanwhile, substantial research had been conducted on aggressive acts by individuals, in couples, in small groups, and in families and community groups.

The prior research had "pretested" the viability of the elements of the aggressive behavior codes. It was, we believed in retrospect, easier to encode the participants' actions from the videotape, stay closer to the information (or data) in wording of the code, and thus get more significant results from the data analysis. Of course, another explanation for the difference in results found was that the research team was not very good at code development or, to be nicer, that we did not do a good job on the development of this code.

Developing a Code Inductively:
A Data-Driven Code

Stage I: Sampling and Design Issues

The steps in developing a code inductively using thematic analysis require, in most cases, criterion-referenced, or anchored, material. The material to be coded must represent a subsample of two or more specific samples used in the research. For example, if you were generating a model of abilities related to performance of managers, you would have a sample of "superior-performing managers" and a sample of "average-performing managers." To develop your ability code, you would need to select a subsample (i.e., three to five people) from each of the two samples. The raw information collected from these two subsamples would be the basis for developing the code. As discussed previously, for example, if critical incident interviews were used as the vehicle of information/data collection, the interview transcripts of these two subsamples could be the basis for developing your desired code of managerial abilities. In situations in which criterion referencing is not possible, as in case studies of one person or organization, a hybrid form of code development is used, which will be discussed later in this chapter.

One of the common dilemmas experienced by researchers, especially early in their career, is that when they are using inductive, or data-driven, approaches to thematic analysis, they have trouble identifying their dependent variable. This is seldom an issue in theory-driven or prior-research-driven approaches to code development. If the study is the first in a series of explorations about a phenomenon, the researcher may not be clear about what type of insight is being sought or why. Without careful thought about the possible dependent variable, or variables, it is difficult to identify a criterion variable as an anchor. Sometimes the criterion variable is one of the independent variables, and the task of criterion referencing is relatively easy.

For example, a researcher wants to study marital conflict. He or she wants to audiotape couples being interviewed about issues in their relationship. If the researcher wants to study factors affecting the degree of conflict in marriages, then he or she has conceptually established degree of conflict as the dependent variable. For data-driven, inductive code development, the researcher will want to identify those couples with relatively high conflict and those with relatively low conflict. This will become the criterion reference and source of subsamples for the code development. If on the other hand, the researcher wants to study male and female differences in discussing marital conflict, using the same interview raw information, he or she is treating gender of the interviewee as the key independent variable. It becomes the criterion reference and source of subsamples for the code development.

Once the researcher has the anchored, or criterion-referenced, material, he or she uses a compare-and-contrast process to extract observable differences between or among the samples. This process, called "immersion and crystallization" by Miller and Crabtree (1992), requires extensive note taking during the processing of the information. Weitzman and Miles (1995) suggested using computers in "memoing" the raw information or using "data linking" and hypertext as a vehicle for encoding the raw information. Mason (1996) described this process as creating categories and then indexing one's raw information to the categories. These are steps on the way to development of an inductively derived, or data-driven, code.

The theoretical meaning of the criterion variables and the rigor with which the criterion sampling (i.e., sampling of persons or events or organizations) is conducted will determine the likelihood of developing a code that can be validated in further studies, as well as the quality of the code. In this sense, the rule of "garbage in, garbage out" will hold for data-driven code development. The quality of the criterion selection and the sampling will determine the quality of the code and subsequently the quality of the findings.

In selecting an appropriate criterion variable or variables for your study, parsimony prevails! For example, selecting gender as your criterion variable will result in your having two criterion groups: men and women. But if you select "age" and you are studying professionals working in a hospital, you will have 10 groups if you split the age range into 5-year segments (i.e., 25-29, 30-34, 35-39, etc.). You will have to cover approximately 25-to 75-year-old professionals. If you are looking for people in different career transitions, a three-way split (i.e., 25-39, 40-55, 56-75) may be meaningful to your inquiry, resulting in three samples to be identified and studied. On the other hand, this split will not help if you are studying retirement patterns, including thoughts about and preparation for retirement.

Multiple criteria complicate your sampling and create an increased work-load during the code development phase of the research. The effect is multi-plicative, not additive!

The raw information, or data, must be in a form that allows easy, repeated review. Written material is easier to review repeatedly than audiotaped or videotaped material. Short segments of audiotaped or videotaped material are easier to review repeatedly than long segments. In code development, you must read, listen, or watch the raw material from the subsamples many times. You may have to review each person's material 8 to 10 times. Rereading a 20-page transcript for each of 10 people is not as easy as rereading a 5-page transcript for each of these people. Careful thought should be given to the selection of the data collection method in terms of the time and energy required to develop the code and later to apply the code to the entire sample.

Sampling of the unit of coding becomes an important concept. For example, if a person is your unit of analysis, your unit of coding may be four critical incidents instead of six to eight incidents, or two staff meetings observed in a month instead of every weekly staff meeting. A discussion of sampling issues can be found in Chapter 3.

Again, as with the theory-driven and prior-research-driven approaches to thematic analysis, there are three stages in developing and using an inductively derived code (see Figure 2.1; also, the comparison of the stages and steps in code development for each of these approaches—theory driven, prior research driven, and data driven—is summarized at the end of this chapter and shown in Table 2.1). With the data-driven, inductive approach to thematic analysis, the first stage not only involves sampling and design for the study but also requires selection of subsamples. (As with sampling, this will be discussed in detail in Chapter 3.) The second stage of code development, in which the researcher discovers and develops themes that differentiate the subsamples, is described in detail below. The third stage of the process, as with the other approaches, involves applying the code (i.e., themes discovered) to the full samples and determining valid differences. Then interpretation is possible.

Stage I: Deciding on sampling and design issues, including selection of the subsamples
Stage II: Developing themes and a code that differentiate the subsamples
Stage III: Applying the code to the full samples to determine valid differences

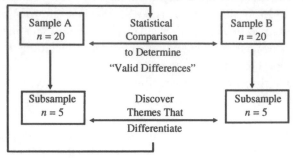

Figure 2.1. Stages in Developing and Using an Inductively Derived Code

Table 2.1 Summary of Stages and Steps in Using Thematic Analysis

Stage	*Theory-Driven Approach*	*Prior-Research-Driven Approach*	*Data-Driven Approach*
I	Deciding on sampling and design issues	Deciding on sampling and design issues	1. Deciding on sampling and design issues 2. Selecting subsamples
II	1. Generating a code from theory 2. Reviewing and rewriting the code for applicability to the raw information 3. Determining the reliability	1. Generating a code from previous research 2. Reviewing and rewriting the code for applicability to the raw information 3. Determining the reliability	1. Reducing the raw information 2. Identifying themes within subsamples 3. Comparing themes across subsamples 4. Creating a code 5. Determining the reliability
III	1. Applying the code to the raw information 2. Determining validity 3. Interpreting results	1. Applying the code to the raw information 2. Determining validity 3. Interpreting results	1. Applying the code to the remaining raw information 2. Determining validity 3. Interpreting results

The reader is reminded that the data-driven, inductive approach is being given considerable space and attention here, not because it is the "best" or even the "recommended" path to code development, but because it is (a) the most fundamental method of developing themes and a code, in the sense that it

(a) Read each protocol entirely.

(b) Create outlines for each protocol.

Alternate (b) Mark source
information by underlining,
making notes, or highlighting
and then outlining

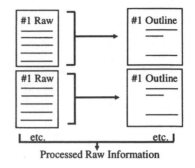

Processed Raw Information

Figure 2.2. Stage II, Step 1: Reducing the Raw Information

requires careful attention to all of the issues and processes used in the other two approaches; (b) the least well understood and least frequently used process for developing codes in many of the social sciences; and (c) the most controversial method from the perspective of journal editors and professional gatekeepers.

Stage II: Developing Themes and a Code

There are five steps involved in inductively developing a code: (a) reducing the raw information, (b) identifying themes within subsamples, (c) comparing themes across subsamples, (d) creating a code, and (e) determining the reliability of the code.

Step 1: Reducing the Raw Information

Read, listen, or watch raw material for *each* unit of analysis, as shown in Figure 2.2. Paraphrase or summarize each piece of data or information. Through these processes, you are entering the information into your unconscious, as well as consciously processing the information. Specifically, (a) read, listen, or watch each protocol (e.g., each transcript); and (b) create an outline of paraphrased items, or a synopsis.

The in-depth review of the material from each unit of analysis in the subsamples provides for close contact and familiarity with the raw informa-

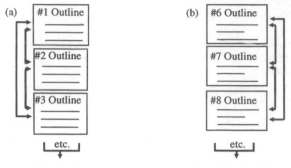

List of Similar Themes   List of Similar Themes

Figure 2.3. Stage II, Step 2: Identifying Themes Within Subsamples

tion. Researchers will often spread the material out in front of them on a large table or even the floor. With written or graphic source material, this often helps them maintain the full picture of the subsample's information.

Step 2: Identifying Themes Within Samples

Compare your summaries to determine similarities among the pieces of information within each subsample, separately, as shown in Figure 2.3. Specifically, (a) compare all of the summaries from one subsample, looking for similarities, or patterns within the subsample (e.g., for patterns within Subjects 1, 2, and 3); and (b) repeat the process for the other subsample.

For material that is relatively short (e.g., a sample of thought that is one paragraph long), the separation of Step 2 and Step 3 is not as clear as it is for most material. For relatively short raw information, such as five paragraphs sampled from five nervous people's thought patterns as compared with five paragraphs sampled from five relaxed people's thought patterns, comparison within and across these two samples (i.e., Steps 2 and 3) could be possible at the same time. But if each person had completed a 1-hour interview, resulting in about 20 to 40 pages of transcript, you would be sampling and analyzing 200 to 400 pages of text! In this situation, Steps 2 and 3 should be approached independently, in the sequence suggested.

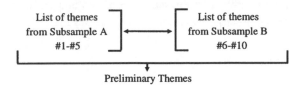

Preliminary Themes

Figure 2.4. Stage II, Step 3: Comparing Themes Across Subsamples

Step 3: Comparing Themes Across Subsamples

Compare the themes, or items, identified as "similar within each group," as shown in Figure 2.4. Compare the two groups through the patterns identified (e.g., compare the similarities seen within Subsample A with the similarities seen within Subsample B).

Although parsimony is a desired characteristic of any thematic code, Steps 2 and 3 are not the time to be terse. At this stage of the process, the aim is to reduce the raw information into smaller "packets." Hopefully, like quantum particles, these "packets" will contain most of the energy of the raw information and be more manageable than the complete raw material.

During Steps 1 through 3, the researcher is busy blocking, inhibiting, or reducing the conceptual interference of his or her own cognitive abilities to formulate concepts while interpreting them. He or she is inhibiting, or attempting to inhibit, the tendency to start the interpretation process (i.e., making sense out of the observed themes). At this point, the focus and energy should be devoted to developing the themes and code. Although the researcher is looking for patterns, and although these patterns must be intellectually coherent, attempts to impose a theoretical framework will result in premature intellectualization. This will lead the researcher into Step 4 with the illusion of a meaningful concept and code. But the code will be more likely to have the characteristics of a theory-driven code than the benefits of a data-driven code.

This is the point in the process at which the researcher is most vulnerable to inner voices of doubt. Like a marathon runner "hitting the wall," the researcher will most likely reach a point in the search for themes distinguishing the two subsamples in which he or she feels that there is nothing to discover. When this occurs, the best advice is to take a break. Talk to others or change perspective, and remind yourself why you are doing the study and why you think the research is important. Once rested and reminded of your purpose, return to the process. Patient perseverance pays!

Step 4: Creating a Code

Write, rewrite, or construct a set of statements that *differentiate* the two groups, or subsamples, as shown in Figure 2.5. This set of preliminary themes is a code. Return to the raw information and reread, listen, or watch the protocols while attempting to determine the presence or absence of each of the preliminary themes. To perform this task, you may have to edit, rewrite, or reconstruct each statement of the preliminary themes into a revised theme, as shown in Figure 2.5. The revised theme may require statements of exclusions in the form of rules for applying the theme to raw material. An example of an exclusion might be, "Do not code this theme as present if the subject is not describing a specific individual. Descriptions of groups of people, even with the language and possible intent of the theme, should not be coded."

Although there are many aspects of a desirable (i.e., usable) code that involve making the code clear, parsimony is another goal. Keeping the objective or research phenomenon in focus is essential in framing a theme and converting it into a code. It is also important to remember that cognitive research continues to support the early observation (Miller, 1956) that humans can typically maintain seven, plus or minus two, variables covarying in their conscious mind at one time. This implies an upper limit to the length and complexity of a usable code. If the coder or observer is to search new raw information for indications of the themes using the code, then he or she must have the code consciously in his or her mind, as well as in front of him or her in some shorthand form. A code with 15 to 20 different themes will inevitably result in coders' "missing" or systematically ignoring items or sets of items. Or it will require reviewing the raw information several times, each time searching for a different aspect of the code (i.e., set of themes). In live observation, this is impossible.

The revised theme should be stated in such a manner that it (a) maximizes the differentiation of the subsamples (i.e., subjects in Group A show it, and subjects in Group B do not show it); (b) facilitates coding of the raw material (i.e., it is easy to apply); and (c) minimizes exclusions. Only those "revised themes" that substantially differentiate the units of analysis of your criterion-referenced subsamples constitute your code. For example, if Revised Theme A differentiates your two subsamples but Revised Theme B does not, you

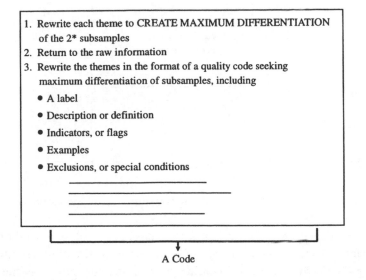

1. Rewrite each theme to CREATE MAXIMUM DIFFERENTIATION of the 2* subsamples
2. Return to the raw information
3. Rewrite the themes in the format of a quality code seeking maximum differentiation of subsamples, including
   - A label
   - Description or definition
   - Indicators, or flags
   - Examples
   - Exclusions, or special conditions

A Code

Figure 2.5. Stage II, Step 4: Creating a Code
*If your criterion variable has more than two categories or levels, then you will have more subsamples.

include Revised Theme A in your code but drop Revised Theme B from further consideration or analysis.

If your criterion variable has more than two categories or levels, you will have more subsamples. You must have one subsample for each category of the criterion variable. For example, developing a code to differentiate the organizational culture of entrepreneurial, growing, mature, and aging organizations would require four subsamples, one from each of the four types of organizations.

Step 5: Determining the Reliability or Consistency of Judgment of the Coders

Apply the code, or themes, to another subsample from your samples. Have another person also apply the code or themes to the same material independently, as shown in Figure 2.6. Calculate your interrater reliability, or determine the degree of consistency of your judgments (see Chapter 7 for more on the issues involved in this step and various methods). Be careful to

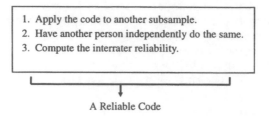

A Reliable Code

Figure 2.6. Stage II, Step 5: Determining the Reliability of the Code

use the appropriate method of computing reliability given the nature of your raw data and code.

If the independent coders cannot achieve desirable levels of reliability or consistency of agreement on any of the themes in the code, you must either (a) drop the theme from further consideration or analysis; or (b) rewrite or reconstruct the theme, and repeat Step 4 above.

The themes for which interrater reliability is achieved can be considered a reliable code, or reliable set of themes.

Stage III: Steps in Validating a Code

Using the code—or at this point in the code development process, it would be more accurate to say "validating the code"—involves two steps.

Step 1: Coding the Rest of the Raw Information

Apply the reliable code to the entire sample, as shown in Figure 2.7.

Step 2: Validating the Code Statistically or Qualitatively

If your raw information and code are appropriate for quantitative analysis, compute the degree to which your samples are statistically differentiated on each of the themes in the reliable code. If your raw information and code are not appropriate for quantitative analysis, visually compare the differentiation on each of your samples in relation to the themes in the reliable code. Those themes showing differentiation constitute your validated code, or validated themes, as shown in Figure 2.8.

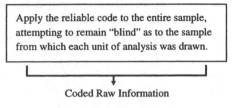

Figure 2.7. Stage III, Step 1: Coding the Raw Information

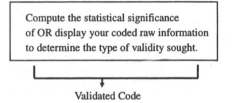

Figure 2.8. Stage III, Step 2: Validating the Code

A researcher may, at this point, question the use of the criterion-referenced subsamples in generating the themes and code. He or she may think it is creating a syllogism. In other words, a colleague might argue that by finding themes that differentiate the subsamples, it is not surprising that they become his or her validated code. The colleague could claim the researcher has used the phenomenon to define itself. The use of the remaining sample of the raw information as a test of the validation is the step that protects the researcher from this possibility. The strength and power of the data-driven approach is that it uses, as much as possible, the way in which the themes appear in the raw information as the starting point in code development. The validation with the entire sample is a cross-check. A further cross-validation study is always desirable to further confirm that the themes identified are not an episodic or idiosyncratic occurrence.

When a Hybrid Approach Is Needed

There are two situations in which a researcher is using a qualitative method and wants to use a data-driven, inductive approach to code development but in which the criterion-referencing method previously described is not possible. In one situation, the study has a single unit of analysis. That is, only one person or organization or family or culture is being studied. In the second situation, the researcher may have multiple units of analysis, but because of either methodological preferences or the nature of the phenomenon, there is no evident or desirable criterion variable. Neither the dependent variable, or consequences of the phenomenon, nor the independent variables constitute an appropriate criterion split for code development.

In such situations, the researcher uses a hybrid of all three approaches. He or she should follow the stages and steps of the inductive, data-driven approach, but without Stage II, Step 3, the comparing and contrasting of themes across the subsamples. That is, the researcher skips Stage II, Step 3, in that process. This forces the researcher into using his or her theories or prior research as a guide for articulation of meaningful themes. Even if the research has not published or consciously articulated his or her theory, he or she probably has one. This hybrid approach relies on these thoughts, ideas, or perceptions more than the data-driven approach does. Of course, these "thoughts, ideas, and perceptions" are typically present even when one is using the data-driven approach, but the compare-and-contrast step should help to minimize any distortion that they might cause.

In case studies of one, there is only one unit of analysis, but there will be multiple units of coding. The compare-and-contrast feature is not possible. This hybrid approach is necessary if the researcher wants to use an inductive approach.

In situations of methodological preference, the person may be attempting to follow a particular qualitative method for which the authors or teachers insist that a comparison is unnecessary or that it violates a premise of their method. In such situations, thematic analysis still contributes by providing a clear set of steps to follow in analyzing the information, standards of a quality code, sensitivity to sampling issues in units of analysis and coding, and ideas about obtaining consistency of judgment (i.e., reliability).

The one application of this hybrid to be avoided occurs when a researcher or graduate student is being lazy. He or she contends that there is no way of identifying a criterion or criteria, thereby thinking to avoid sampling issues. Sometimes, the "laziness" emerges from confusion about the phenomenon or not having thought it through carefully. On these occasions, a person can pursue a project but should not consider it research of a standard and quality that merits dissemination to others. Again, this does not mean that any researcher not wanting to use the compare-and-contrast step of the data-driven approach to code development is being lazy. Quite the contrary: In the early stages of exploration of phenomenon, often so little is known or understood that even articulating a dependent variable or appropriate independent variable is difficult. There are also times at which the researcher is seeking to describe a person, group, culture, or event. Thematic analysis helps in making that description clearer and in making the themes or code developed potentially useful to other researchers. The point of this warning is that qualitative research has too often been abused by those who have made it an excuse for sloppy or illogical research. Hopefully, through publication and training in various qualitative methods (and the use of thematic analysis with those methods!), the richness of qualitative research will become a socially acceptable, professionally credible technique for generating insight.

Review of the Approaches and Characteristics of a Quality Code

A summary of the stages and steps in the three approaches to using thematic analysis is shown in Table 2.1 earlier in this chapter.

To review, a *"good" code* should have five elements:

1. A label (i.e., a name)
2. A definition of what the theme concerns (i.e., the characteristic or issue constituting the theme)
3. A description of how to know when the theme occurs (i.e., indicators on how to "flag" the theme)
4. A description of any qualifications or exclusions to the identification of the theme
5. Examples, both positive and negative, to eliminate possible confusion when looking for the theme.

CHAPTER THREE

Deciding on Units
of Analysis and Units
# of Coding as Issues of Sampling

Thematic analysis is sensitive to the quality of the raw data or information. Therefore, sampling decisions not only affect but to a large extent determine the degree of reliability and validity attainable. Beyond the usual concerns of generalizing from a sample to a population, sampling decisions will affect thematic analysis in the consistency or reliability of judgments attainable. Because qualitative methods are often used in early stages of inquiry and to examine unusual or complex phenomena, the degree to which the raw information represents the phenomenon becomes an interpretive dilemma requiring theoretical as well as empirical support or justification for the sample studied.

Types of Sampling

As with all research, before deciding what information to collect and about whom, the researcher must clarify the population of interest. General concepts influencing generalizability from a sample to a population apply to any qualitative method. Sometimes researchers or graduate students choosing qualitative methods claim that the specific method chosen does not imply generalization but merely offers description. The reader is left to read the work as a case study of one, like a novel or poem, and allow it to stimulate thoughts, conclusions, or generalizations as the reader wishes. Although various epistemologies address and emphasize generalizability in considerably different ways, once you offer something to others, especially through written or electronic communication in which you are not present to add qualifications, you have an ethical responsibility to not mislead readers. Of course, one can never prevent readers from engaging in abusive or irresponsible interpretation, but a scholar can take responsibility to minimize the likelihood of misinterpretation. The adequacy and appropriateness of the sample as regards the larger population, whether of individuals, organizations, cultures, or events, is in the hands, heart, and mind of the researcher before collecting information.

Although random sampling increases the likelihood of sound generalizations to the population, it is not always feasible and is often too cumbersome. Patton (1990) described the alternatives to random sampling as 16 specific types of purposive sampling:

> extreme or deviant case sampling; intensity sampling; maximum variation sampling; homogeneous sampling; typical case sampling; stratified purposeful sampling; critical case sampling; snowball or chain sampling; criterion sampling; theory-based or operational construct sampling; confirming and disconfirming cases; opportunistic sampling; random purposeful sampling; sampling politically important cases; convenience sampling; and combination or mixed sampling. (pp. 182-183)

To avoid duplication of Patton's (1990) excellent discussion of sampling and research design, we will look at critical issues in making specific sampling decisions once the researcher's overall research design has been selected. Mason (1996) also has an excellent discussion of sampling and selection issues.

In thematic analysis, three types of sampling are of critical importance: sampling the criterion or dependent variable, sampling subjects, and sampling the raw material. Four types of sampling may affect the dependent variable, criterion, or phenomenon of interest: setting, events, people, and relationships. Each type of sampling must be considered regarding the unit of analysis *and* the unit of coding.

Setting

The phenomenon of interest occurs in a context, or setting. The sampling questions are:

1. Does the context, or setting, have a significant impact on the phenomenon of interest in terms of our ability to obtain a comprehensive picture of it?
2. Does the context, or setting, have a significant impact on the phenomenon of interest in terms of our ability to generalize the results of our analysis?

For example, one possible framework for sampling by setting may be categorized as specific, organizational, or large-scale settings. A *specific setting* could be a monthly staff meeting, a neighborhood bar on Friday night, or a manager giving a subordinate performance feedback. This setting has physical as well as social and political characteristics.

An *organizational setting* could be a company, such as IBM; a city agency, such as the Cleveland Heights Police Department; a professional association, such as the American Psychological Association; or the 4H Club. Often, entities within an organization, such as divisions of General Electric, or a marketing department, are important to consider as organizational settings.

A *large-scale setting* could be a country, such as Italy; a cultural group, such as the Kurdish people; or a philosophical or religious orientation, such as existentialists or Hindus.

The setting may even be nested within other important settings. For example, suppose you are studying decision making in the Catholic churches of northeastern Ohio. You must consider the large-scale religious and political setting of the Catholic Church, given that the Vatican and the local diocese have a potential impact on decision making. You must consider the organizational setting: Which specific churches will you select to study? Should they be both urban and rural? Should they be churches in communities in which Catholics constitute a large or a small proportion of the local population? You must consider which specific events in the life of a specific church to observe and document as your raw information. Do you study the priest's thought process of sermon selection, budget meetings with staff, or board meetings?

Events

Sampling by events can be categorized as sampling by time, by regular social occurrences, or by special occasions/events. *Times* to be sampled could include various times of the day, such as mornings, afternoons, and evenings; days of the week, such as Tuesday night and Saturday night; or months and seasons of the year, such as summer and winter months. Again, adequacy in representing the richness of the phenomenon *and* generalizability to the population that the sample represents are important considerations in any of the sampling issues.

Another important influence of time is in the potential difficulty of finding consistent information for criterion sampling. For example, suppose you want to study gender relationships as depicted in popular movies in the 1940s versus the 1960s versus the 1980s. To select the appropriate films to view for the thematic analysis, you want to select those films viewed by the most people in movie theaters. Attending a movie theater requires a decision to go to a specific film. If many people go, it can be claimed that the images in the film are of interest and probably reflect the values, desires, or mood of the viewers at the time. But which measure do you use? Box office receipts should be adjusted for inflation. But were such statistics kept with the same diligence in the 1940s as in the 1980s? Distributors may have kept records of the number of times a movie was shown, which you might use as a measure of popularity. But in the 1980s, with multiplex theaters and reduced personnel inside movie theaters, chains show films even if no one is in the audience. Also, by the 1980s, you have to decide how to calculate the people watching the film at home with their VCR; by the late 1980s, some movies were being released in video format within 6 months of theater release! That was not done in the late 1970s or even the early 1980s.

Regular social occurrences could include meals, morning prayers, or monthly staff meetings. If the basis of the regularity of such events is time, then event sampling based on time will address the variations of regular social occurrences. For example, breakfast occurs in the morning for many people. But those working evening shifts, entertainers, and graduate students who have adapted to "all-nighters" may eat breakfast at 7:00 p.m.

If the regular social occurrence varies over time, then both issues should be considered. For example, if you were studying people's self-esteem on their birthdays, you would probably want to sample people in their teens, 20s, and 30s as part of regular social occurrence sampling. You would also want to consider people with January, April, July, and October birthdays as part of time sampling. It gets complicated. Even here, if you believed in astrology, or thought that your subjects might, you would change the sampling by time in terms of adding people from each of the 12 signs of the zodiac.

A *special occasion* could be a one-time unique event, such as the Woodstock musical extravaganza, the 1968 Democratic National Convention in Chicago, the onset of the Depression, or the assassination of Martin Luther King, Jr. It could also be an event extending over a long time period, such as the coronation in Britain or the unification of Germany.

People

Sampling by people means including different people with regard to any characteristic of concern. For example, a study of people's views on marriage should include men and women, as well as heterosexuals and homosexuals, if one is to generalize results to "people." It would be misleading to study views of death without considering people at different ages, people who have experienced a close relative or friend's death, and people with and without life-threatening diseases such as cancer, AIDS, or diabetes.

If I want to understand adolescents' views of death, adolescents are the population to which I wish to generalize. My sample will include adolescents but may include other age groups as well. To borrow a concept from photography, I may want to "bracket" the sample. In photography, *bracketing* refers to the practice of taking several photographs of the same scene with exposures at the supposedly ideal setting, as well as one or two f-stops above and below it. That is, I may want to interview not only adolescents but also younger children and young adults to generate comparative information. These groups provide a conceptual context and, in a sense, a bracket for the group I wish to study.

Because providing information for qualitative research often involves asking a person for more time than completing a questionnaire, and given appropriate ethical concerns for informed consent and volition in participation, often people are asked to volunteer. A sample of volunteers is potentially contaminated with all of the factors that have been shown to be distinctive about volunteers versus random samples of individuals from various populations (Rosenthal & Rosnow, 1969).

Relationships

Sampling by relationships should consider structure, affect, and purposes of the relationships. The *structure* of relationships refers to the size and composition of relationships, such as pairs, trios, nuclear families, or small groups. *Affect,* or mood, of relationships should be considered in sampling. For example, in studying commitment of work teams to an organization, it may be important to examine both work teams in fast-growth organizations with an optimistic view of the future and work teams in organizations that have experienced recent layoffs or downsizing.

The *purpose,* or nature, of the relationship should be considered in sampling. For example, studying types of communication among small groups of five people should consider the potential differences among five people in a variety of settings. For example, to fully understand communication among five-person small groups, we might want to study a Saturday morning "pickup" basketball game, five siblings planning a family event, and the crew of a space shuttle mission.

Tests of the Sampling Design

The sampling design of research studies using thematic analysis should be tested for adequacy and appropriateness with regard to its efficacy, efficiency, and ethics. The adequacy and appropriateness will, in large part, be determined by the particular project's stage in the research of the phenomenon. For example, thematic analysis is often used in the exploratory or discovery stage of a study. Sampling issues are elusive at this point of a research effort. Given the lack of understanding of the phenomenon of interest, or dependent variable, multiple studies may be required merely to identify significant sampling issues.

In this way, the appropriateness of the sampling design will depend on the stage of research. Without a substantial prior research literature on which to base sampling designs, the creativity found in diverse or pluralistic perspectives will be essential.

Efficacy

One can assess the efficacy of the sampling design by answering at least the following two questions:

1. Is there sufficient variety of types of *units of analysis* to allow for analysis of "between-unit" variance and therefore generalization?
2. Is there sufficient variety of types of *units of coding* to allow for a comprehensive understanding and analysis of the unit of analysis?

Testing the efficacy of the sampling anticipates rival hypotheses, contaminants, and confusion that otherwise might surface in the data analysis and interpretation segments of the study.

The efficacy of the design will determine the complexity of data collection and time requirements. This issue is particularly important for studies using thematic analysis because the number of units of analysis to be sampled will be multiplied by the number of units of coding to yield the number of "data points" to be analyzed.

Given the nature of the material analyzed with thematic analysis, the coding time is often a multiple of the time involved in collecting the information. For example, coding of videotapes of five to eight people for abilities demonstrated by each person will typically require two times the running time of the videotape. If you were studying the emergence of group process abilities in five-person quality circles, you would want at least 1 hour of videotape from each quality circle from one each of its early, middle, and late sessions. Even if you limited your study to manufacturing divisions of chemical companies and you were in a discovery stage, it would be desirable to study three different quality circles from each of five different companies.

That means, you would *begin* such a study with 45 hours of videotape. One hour from each quality circle early, middle, and late in its life would mean 3 hours per quality circle; three different quality circles from a division, each requiring 3 hours, would mean 9 hours of tape per division; and five different companies, each requiring 9 hours, would mean 45 hours of tape. Assuming that you were using a thematic code developed elsewhere, you would be committing yourself to at least about 90 hours of coding time. This, of course, does not consider the possibility of needing to have another person code (called *double coding*) the videotapes, resulting in 180 hours of coding time!

Efficiency

Whether you double-code or seek to establish interrater reliability among several people coding the raw data in some other way (see the discussion in Chapter 7), the time requirements will grow beyond the time to view the videotapes in a multiplicative manner. You can see why efficiency becomes a crucial test of sampling design. You can use sampling to make the coding time manageable. For instance, using this example, you might decide to study only companies without a prior emphasis on group process. That is, you might choose to study only those companies with a vision statement or culture description requiring attendance at company-sponsored training programs. Because everyone in the company would be attending group training programs regularly, you could make the assumption that the employees were accustomed to working in groups. Therefore, you might expect the participants engaged in the quality circles not to change noticeably in their behavior associated with group functioning. The expectation of only small changes might preclude the need for the middle time period of videotaping. This decision would reduce the coding time to 60 hours, or 120 hours if you were double-coding.

Ethics

Testing the adequacy of the sampling design regarding ethics leads to another set of concerns. The raw data or information collected for studies using thematic analysis is a person's own words, or actions, or observable aspects of his or her life in an organization. This often results in relatively "more sensitive" raw data than are usually collected with questionnaires or surveys. The increased sensitivity requires a high degree of thought and caution regarding the subject's informed consent, protection of confidentiality, protection against abusive use of raw or coded data, and protection against abusive application of the results of the study.

For example, if you were studying the culture within an organization, you might use a Likert-scaled climate survey. It would ask people to describe their views of the atmosphere within the organization by checking a box indicating whether they strongly disagreed, disagreed, agreed, or strongly agreed. Once the questionnaires were completed by the staff in one department, the scores on the items in the questionnaire would be compiled into scale scores, and the scale scores would be averaged for all of the staff. So in response to a set of items describing the atmosphere within the department as having a great deal of fairness in the distribution of rewards and recognition, an average score of 1.63 would indicate that the employees disagreed with the statement. If the results were presented to the organization's management and employees as a "thank you" for the right to collect the data for research, a vindictive manager would not be able to identify a person who said such nasty things.

But suppose that you have chosen to study the same climate in the organization by interviewing people with open-ended questions. In attempting to determine the fairness of rewards and recognition, you may ask, "Are rewards and recognition given to people in this organization? And how?" You audiotape the interviews. After analyzing your information for your research, you compile themes observed for a "feedback" session to management and the employees and present your results with all present.

Conscientiously, you use quotes to illustrate people's statements—without identifying the person, of course. One quote is: "The best assignments are given to the boss's favorites. Those people that flatter him all the time. Doing a good job isn't the issue here, it's brown-nosing the managers that gets you noticed. Staying quiet and keeping your head down is the play!" Just as you are reading this quote, two of the employees in the audience start to whisper and seem agitated. The manager knows that one of them uses the phrase "brown-nose" a lot. Confidentiality has now been breached, and an unintended consequence of your study may be an employee's getting fired or harassed.

The possibility of sources being identified from written or audiotaped information is significant. From videotaped information, of course, it is certain. To protect the confidentiality of the people providing the information, you must not allow anyone other than the research team to view the tapes. It might make the presentation of your results more interesting to show segments of the videotapes, but people can be identified! If individual confidentiality has been assured, then people other than the researcher or research team cannot view the tapes.

The Unit of Analysis
Versus the Unit of Coding

As with most types of social science research, in research using thematic analysis, the unit of coding is usually different from the unit of analysis. In a questionnaire-based study comparing organizational climate of various types of social service agencies, the unit of coding would be the questionnaire item, whereas the unit of analysis would be the organization. With the use of thematic analysis, the unit of coding is a complex and sometimes confusing issue.

Unit of Analysis

The unit of analysis is the entity on which the interpretation of the study will focus. To clarify the unit of analysis, the researcher could ask him- or herself these questions: How will I organize the results section of my research paper or report? How will I construct the tables or organize the text to present the findings? If the study is exploring the relationship between aspects of an organization's culture and its financial performance, the unit of analysis is the organization. In the interpretation section of the report of the study, we can expect the authors to make statements such as "Organizations with a culture emphasizing their pride and distinctiveness in the marketplace appear to generate higher returns on capital employed than do organizations with a culture emphasizing efficiency and market dominance." The authors are describing differences between two groups of organizations.

The type of information collected both affects and is affected by the unit of analysis. For instance, if your information is samples of thought, as in the case of an autobiographical essay or a videotape of people making presentations, you are likely to have a person as the unit of analysis. If your information is audiotapes or videotapes of small groups working on a task, your unit of analysis could be the person, relationships such as dyads, or the group as a whole. If you have observational records of street gangs, the way in which you record the information will determine whether you have to use the gang as the unit of analysis. If you have recorded your observations by specific person, then you have the option of also using the person as the unit of analysis. When using historical documents, such as songs, hymns, memos, journals, and such, you must determine whether each item can be identified with a specific individual; if it cannot, the individual cannot be the unit of analysis.

Unit of Coding

The unit of coding is the most basic segment, or element, of the raw data or information that can be assessed in a meaningful way regarding the phenomenon. The unit of coding can never be an entity larger than the unit of analysis. For example, suppose you are studying the relationship between task performance and a person's affective response. You want the unit of analysis to be the individual. Let us assume that the task is performed by a team and that you are using a thematic code to determine the degree of positive or negative affect expressed. If you apply the code to the group's affect, saying that the particular group under observation was feeling good about their performance on the last task, it would be difficult to then interpret or even infer that a particular individual in the group felt good about the task accomplishment. You would have to apply the code person by person to interpret or infer that a specific individual felt good about the task performance. In this case, you would have made the person the unit of coding.

The unit of coding determines the comprehensiveness of your insight into the unit of analysis. For example, suppose that you are studying the affective response of individuals to a Michael Jackson concert as compared to the affective response of individuals to a concert by the Boston Symphony Orchestra. You might sample individuals' reactions immediately following the concert and 2 weeks after the concert. Assume that your raw data were collected by audiotaping individuals' responses to several questions, such as "How did you feel about the concert?" Let us also assume that you are using a thematic code for types of affect and intensity of affect. Because your study is comparing affective responses of individuals to the concerts, the individual is the unit of analysis.

If you define a "sustained affective reaction" as one in which a person's intensity of affective reaction drops no more than 50% in the 2 weeks following the concert, your unit of coding must be each interview. You must determine, through coding, a person's reaction immediately following the concert. Then you must make another independent determination of the person's reaction 2 weeks later. Each of those interviews or segments of audiotape must be coded. Therefore, the interview is the unit of coding.

The unit of coding is significantly affected by the nature of the raw data, or information. If the raw data are people's written responses to open-ended questions, the unit of coding could be (listed in order of descending size) the entire response, the response to each question, the paragraph, or the sentence. If the raw data are audiotaped responses, the unit of coding could be determined by the structure of the interview (e.g., by each question), by the linguistic segments (e.g., by each sentence), or by time (e.g., by 5-minute segments of audiotape).

When historical documents are the source material, questions about the unit of coding are the most complex (Holsti, 1968; Winter, 1992). If you are coding speeches, myths, or popular fiction, efficiency of the sampling of units of coding becomes a concern. McClelland (1974) recommended coding 100-line segments and enough randomly sampled segments to ensure coding of at least 10% of the words in a book or hymn or myth. Winter and Healy (1981) described a method for coding "running text" in which the sentence becomes the unit of coding.

The unit of coding should have a theoretical justification, given the phenomenon of interest and the unit of analysis, and should provide the opportunity to establish and observe a "codable moment." Suppose that you were studying the impact of self-confidence on risk taking and that your theoretical definition of self-confidence included the observation that a person "consistently demonstrates an unhesitating, forceful, assured manner." Your "theory" would require multiple observations of the individual. Each observation would be a unit of coding. If you were using a comprehensive personality theory, your observations (i.e., units of coding) would have to include information about the person at home, at work, and at leisure.

The unit of coding must be chosen to provide sufficient opportunity for a "codable moment" within the type of raw information. In the example of the study about self-confidence, observing a person at home while taking a nap, reading, or watching television, no matter how many hours of videotape or direct observation might be involved, might not provide the opportunity to see the person with other people, which would be required, given the definition of self-confidence being used.

Linking Units of Coding and Analysis to the Phenomenon

Description and explanation of units of coding and units of analysis make the process of selecting them sound logical and rational. It does not always appear that way when you are designing a study or in the middle of making sense of your data. As with most research, any of the methods used becomes clearer with experience and practice. Because the units of coding and analysis and the process of interpreting the phenomenon are interconnected, it is easy to get confused.

Many graduate students in psychology learned to refine their skills in identifying rival hypotheses and designing research to control for certain variables through design of laboratory experiments. Then some learned to "loosen up" and use quasi-experimental designs with Campbell and Stanley (1963) as their guide. In the same way, first-time travelers to Europe 60 years ago would not have left home without their *Baedeker* travel guide, but after a number of trips, they would create their own guidebooks and pass them among friends and colleagues. Today, entire bookstores are devoted to travel guides! So it is with sampling and design issues in qualitative studies. Most researchers currently using thematic analysis learned design and sampling by apprenticing themselves to others to learn the craft. Today, there are many books and guides to these issues in qualitative methods. When the researcher chooses to use thematic analysis to process and understand his or her information, units of analysis and coding become crucial to distinguish.

A useful exercise while in the early stages of developing or refining your research skills (and not a bad discipline for the experienced researcher) is to look for what might be "left out" of your information. Once you have determined the units of analysis, units of coding, and data collection method, ask yourself repeatedly, "What aspects of the phenomenon might not be noted,

TABLE 3.1   Examples of Units of Analysis, Units of Coding, and the Related
                 Phenomenon of Interest

Phenomenon of Interest	Unit of Analysis	Unit of Coding
Individual change	Person	Sample of behavior
	Person	An essay describing one's mood or one's reaction to an event
Individual abilities	Person	Critical incident
	Person	A group exercise
Group development	Group	Early, middle, and late samples of the group's functioning
Coalitions	Group	Interactions
Coalition membership	Individual	Each person's interactions with others
Reference group identity	Group	Stories that group members tell about the group
Interpersonal relationships	Dyads	An exchange of actions/interactions
Organizational cultural	Organization	Observed events, such as staff meetings
Cultural differences	Culture	Myths or folktales

observable, or available for processing with this design?" Present your design
and decisions to colleagues, and ask them to critique it. Can they think of
anything you might have overlooked?

In pilot-testing your methods, look for anomalies. If something about the
information does not fit in the picture, such as a person answering a question
in a way you had not considered possible, note the anomaly. Examine it and
decide whether it is revealing some element you had not considered but should
have considered.

Table 3.1 offers some examples of units of coding and units of analysis
in relation to the underlying concept or phenomenon of curiosity.

As suggested earlier in the book, some methods of recording information—
for example, comparing videotapes versus written transcripts of the same
events—result in better, more complete information but can cause problems
in the analysis. Videotapes offer multiple channels of information—content
from the audio channel, tone from the audio channel, nonverbal cues from the
video channel, and observed interactions—whereas the written transcripts
eliminate the nonverbal and severely limit the information about interactions
and tone. But these extra channels of rich information can easily overwhelm
the coder. Designing the unit of coding to suit the type of information is
essential.

CHAPTER FOUR

Developing Themes and a Code Using the Inductive Method

An Example Using Life Stories

ife stories, sometimes called *biodata* or *autobiographical data*, have a social history dating back to hunting and gathering tribes sitting around campfires. Telling stories about one's past experiences and events was a method of communicating emotions, transmitting cultural values, and creating a history. (Besides that, sometimes it was fun!) More recently, life stories have been used by social scientists in a variety of ways (Coffey & Atkinson, 1996). Dailey (1971) adapted techniques used by Haldane and associates in career counseling to assess a person's strengths and weaknesses. Through analysis of these patterns in one's life events, Dailey constructed tests to assist in the assessment of various competencies. McAdams (1985) explored use of life histories with regard to power and intimacy motives in the McClelland (1985) tradition and the extension of the themes noted to the construction of people's identities. There is even a journal, the *Journal of Narrative Life Stories,* that focuses on the use of this technique.

The Life Story Exercise

In examining how people developed various competencies, Dreyfus (1990) first had to establish which competencies and other characteristics differentiated high-performing managers from their less effective counterparts. Nominations from supervisors, peers, and subordinates were used as the information from which to make the criterion sampling decisions. The nomination form presented a blank sheet and asked for the names of any current managers, at a specified level in the organization, whom the respondent "considered to be most effective in their current role as a manager." Those managers who repeatedly appeared on nomination forms from all three levels were classified as highly effective managers. Those managers who received no nominations from any of the three levels were classified as typical performers.

In this study, one of the instruments used was the Life Story Exercise, a self-administered questionnaire adapting various questions from McAdams (1985). Dreyfus's dissertation, entitled *The Characteristics of High Performing Managers of Scientists and Engineers* (1990), includes full documentation of the methods and analysis. The managers were given 1 hour to write answers to four life story questions. The researchers collecting the information were "blind" to the criterion group membership of the managers in the sample.

The Life Story Exercise asked the person to respond to the following four questions (Dreyfus, 1990). Each of the questions appeared at the top of a separate page, with an extra page provided for the first question.

> 1) Think of your life (past, present and future) as if it were a book. Most books are divided into chapters. Each chapter tells a kind of story; that is, it has a plot. Think about this, then divide your life into chapters, give each chapter a name and for each provide a short plot summary (i.e., two-four sentences). Try to think about the major events in your life as "turning points" leading from one chapter to the next.
>
> 2) Many people report occasional "peak experiences." These are generally moments or episodes in a person's life in which he or she feels a sense of transcendence, breakthrough, uplifting, and inner peace. These experiences vary widely. Some people report them to be associated with religious experiences. Others may find such a "high" in vigorous athletics, reading a good novel, an intellectual insight, artistic expression, working with a team to complete an innovative project, or simply talking with a good friend.
>
> Please describe in four to five sentences something akin to a peak experience that you have experienced. Please be specific. Include what happened, who was there, how it felt, what you were thinking, and how (if at all) the experience changed you.

3) A "nadir" is a low point. A nadir experience, then, is the opposite of a peak experience. Please think of your life. Try to remember a specific experience in which you felt a sense of disillusionment and/or despair. This would be one of the low points in your life. Even though this memory is undoubtedly unpleasant, please be specific (four to five sentences) and report as much detail as you did for the peak experience.

4) In thinking about your life, who has had an important impact on your development? Who have been significant role models? Please list these individuals by name and write a sentence or two describing the impact each has had on your development. (pp. 34-35)

Selected actual life stories are presented here as an opportunity to demonstrate the process of developing a thematic code inductively. To be specific, this is Stage II of the data-driven, or inductive, approach to developing a code. The reader can use this as an exercise. Following the steps described in the previous chapter, read the following six life stories and see if you can develop a thematic code. You can then compare your analysis and code development to my own and Dreyfus's. This is not to say that ours are the only or even the "best" thematic analysis and codes that can be developed from this material. They are offered for purposes of the illustration and comparison if you choose to engage in the exercise.

The Subsample

A subsample of 3 of the 17 superior-performing managers and a subsample of 3 of the 17 typical-performing managers were randomly selected from the sample, as described in Chapter 2 (see Figure 2.2). Names and dates have been changed, but everything else appears as it did on their original handwritten responses.

Stage II, Step 1: Reducing the Raw Information

The objectives of Step 1 are to understand the raw information, internalize as much of it as possible (i.e., bring it into conscious functioning and at least medium-term memory), and reduce it to a manageable size. Reducing the raw information may not result in fewer pages or fewer lines but will give it a shortened "outline" form, easier for comparison across units of analysis—in this case, individuals.

Two common difficulties with this step are that the researcher may prematurely identify themes and that he or she may become fatigued. With information such as life stories, a researcher typically spends several hours trying to make sense of it. Each step helps to reduce the likelihood of information overload and feelings of futility. Researchers new to thematic analysis often report having the sense that there is nothing in the data, nothing to differentiate criterion samples or capture the essence of the case study. This sense of foreboding dissipates with time. Patience and determination are, therefore, important personal characteristics to be encouraged and used at this step in the process. The steps in this process can be used both to prevent premature theme identification and to counter the fear that nothing will emerge from the information.

Outlines can take many forms. In the following pages, one is offered as an example. Key activities, affect, thoughts, and emotions will be considered as potential themes in the outline of these life stories. These types of items are selected as particularly relevant because the inquiry is about individual abilities or competencies, and we are examining raw information from brief autobiographical statements.

Again, the reader is encouraged to use this example as an exercise in developing or at least practicing the development of a thematic code.

Manager 1: Typical Performer

1) 1. *Infancy*—I was born Feb 3, 1946 or so they tell me. I don't know for sure as I do not remember my birth. My first recollection was playing.

2. *Glorious Childhood Days*—I had a great time playing with my sisters, neighborhood friends, and class mates. The number of playmates decreased when we moved to the country when I was 5 years old. However the "great out of doors" opened up a new play arena for me until my "teenage years" really began at 14.

3. *The Golden Days*—is the title I give to my teenage years because there were so many fun things to do. The reason I said my "teenage years" began at 14 is I was 14 when I discovered girls. My life has never been the same since. High school and college were almost the same until February 23, 1968, my wedding day.

4. *First Marriage*—It was on that day that my life really changed. Suddenly responsibilities were there. (Not many, but there just the same.) I was still in school, undergrad. And then graduate school for oh so long. . . . As the years of grad school trudged on so did the relationship. Sadness crept in, followed by despair, my medical problems—blindness and worse.

5. *Single Again*—She left. It was over and final, quickly in 6 months. I was numb but starting to live a little.

6. *Barbara*—She came into my life in a big way. She too was hurting and together we learned to live again. PhD, vows of marriage, a real job and a family. Life can be good.

7. *Job, No Career*—Demanding and challenging satisfaction.

2) A peak experience that comes to mind was when I was first asked to consider going into management by Harry Benson. Harry, who is my boss, asked me if I would apply for my present position. I felt greatly honored as this indicated that I was highly thought of as a researcher and a person at Molecule Inc. Since being selected for the position my life has become difficult, as this is not an easy job.

3) A real low point in my life was the day I returned home to find that my first wife had left. "I need to get away for a few day to think" the note said. It was the next day when she returned home that I realized she had spent the weekend with someone else. All I remember was what she was wearing when she returned—and how much it hurt.

4) My Aunt Agnes—my fourth grade teacher and occasionally mother substitute. She always said "You can get the job done, just "buckle-down" to it."

Miss Susan Winston—Always expected me to do my best.

My father—Frank Simpson—the perfect example of perseverance.

My mother—Betty Simpson—Always loving.

My wife—Barbara—Always caring.

Manager 2: Typical Performer

1) *School Years*

I was shy, but not overly withdrawn. Much more fascinated with things and making them work (or seeing how they worked) than in interacting with people. I was also quite religious and impressed with my obligations to it. Typically had a few class friends, changing with time.

College

Opening up in terms of horizons. I became disillusioned with teachings on religion, and joined a fraternity and worked at becoming a socialite. After my freshman year, I decided that I wanted to make the time pay and went into physics adding rigor to my technical interests of old. Continued into graduate school and got very specialized. Social life went well during this time. Met my future wife and married.

Early Molecule Inc.

Although I intended to go into college teaching, an ROTC commission and some luck brought me to Molecule, Inc. where they were doing similar work. I was made a manager of the group after less than two years, but remained doing research for 8 more with management as a side activity.

Diaspora

Cutbacks at Molecule, Inc. resulted in the abolition of our research effort. I was offered a position managing on-line data acquisition. I have since changed positions several times, mostly because of project changes, but a couple of times on my own. Goals have mostly to do important work, but also to avoid career traps.

2) I once built a very complicated nuclear experiment based on theory and which took several months of effort. It was exhilarating to see the data come in on the scope exactly (and somewhat magically) just as the arcane theory said it should. It was shared by other members of the team but they didn't see the significance. I think that the main impact on me was the affirmation that complex enterprises *can* work if they are done right.

3) One of the worst experiences was learning that our research effort would be terminated for budgetary reasons on the same day we completed and successfully tested the Molecule, Inc. _____ [name of a machine] after a 2½ year design and construction program. The irony and the lack of any appeal were very disheartening.

4) There are two types of important people:

1. Those who influenced me over a long period of time, but not in clearly specific ways.

2. Those who changed my thinking by a single comment or act.

For the latter

I worked a summer job as a teenager with a H.S. shop teacher named "Joe" Joseph. He taught me to listen to others.

A college professor astounded me by cheerfully admitting "I don't know" on several occasions—taught emotional honesty.

For the former

My Grandmother—was a very dynamic woman who showed me how to get things done and to be positive.

W. B. McGraw—a Professor Emeritus was an inspiring role model.

My Wife—who is an artist and quite different has helped round out my personality.

A couple of acting instructors who showed me a different way of thinking.

Manager 3: Typical Performer

1) *School Days*

Covers elementary through grad school. Fairly successful in academic pursuits. Major problem was a speech impediment, which tended to make me hover in background rather than seek limelight.

Early Career/Marriage

Left home to seek fortune and fame. Married and started family. Successful in first job, but I left organization when plant closed. Another year in grad school.

Molecule Career—First Half

Very successful and satisfying. Very technically productive. Appointed supervisor after being on job only three years. Supervisory duties occupied very little time so I could continue my technical work.

Molecule—Second Half

Transferred to a new project organization and then went through a few job changes. Supervisor duties taking more time. Not as satisfying as when I was technically productive.

Retirement

I become eligible for early retirement in about 1 ½ years. Looking forward to retiring from Molecule and returning to purely technical work in another setting. Children all out of school by this time.

2) This is not a single peak experience, but an activity. I very much enjoy teaching. Getting up in front of a class and lecturing gives me a high (perhaps it's an ego trip). I enjoy explaining complex technical subjects in simple understandable terms. I like to see the "light bulbs" turn on as understanding comes to the students.

3) There was a reorganization in which four managers in one organization lost their positions. I was one of these. We received no reasonable explanation for this action. I was a Department Manager at the time. It was very disheartening. I was "kicked out" of the area where I had established my technical reputation and moved to a non-supervisory staff job in another organization. Now, thinking of this, my "single" peak experience was making it back to a managerial position three years later.

4) *My parents*—they taught me to be honest and caring in dealing with others. They encouraged me to pursue my goals.

Joshua Brent—my first supervisor at Molecule. He taught me the polymer business. He was always there with answers to questions. He taught me how to interact with upper management. He was the motivating force behind many of my technical accomplishments during these years.

Manager 4: Superior Performer

1) 1. Pre-college

A single life with little knowledge of the world or what opportunities were available. Very limited expectations as to my station in life and little idea of what I wanted to do.

2. College

First real step in maturation both from a personal and profession viewpoint. A developing awareness of my capabilities and some ideas as to what I wanted to do with at least my career. Limited confidence in my capabilities.

3. First Ten Years of Work

Blissful happiness with my work. Plenty of money, lots of freedom, isolated from the realities of budgets, etc. by my supervisors. Limited career expectations because reality already exceeded original dreams.

4. Next Ten Years of Work

Growing awareness of my abilities to take an active role in steering my career as well as the future of the organization. Probably overconfidence set in. Established rather high expectations as to what I could accomplish and contribute. A feeling that I could contribute more as a manager than as an individual researcher.

5. Post First Twenty Years Until Present

The development of a more pragmatic viewpoint probably spawned by frustrations in limited resources to do a job that I feel is very important. A sense of being overwhelmed by responsibilities. A deep sense of concern for the people in my Department as I watch them struggle to do more with less.

2) I don't think I've really reached/experienced what I would classify as a "peak experience." I've had plenty of events which have been fulfilling but I guess I'm still waiting for that "peak." The only real memories which really stand out in my mind revolve around my family (i.e., wife and kids).

3) Probably the lowest points in my life have revolved around those events that have reminded me of my inherent mortality or many weaknesses. For example, when I was diagnosed as possibly having high blood pressure it was very hard for me to accept because it demonstrated a fragility in my life that I didn't want to think about.

4) Only one person here at Molecule has really had what I consider a profound influence on my career. That person is Dave Manser who was first my Project Leader and then my Department Manager. He *forced* me to expand my thinking beyond my individual career and activities. In a period of less than a year, my whole perspective on what I wanted to do changed and I still admire him for opening my eyes to a whole new career.

Manager 5: Superior Performer

1) I. Establishing the Foundation for Independence

I began the education process for my life's work and the process of establishing independence as a self-sufficient adult. Undergraduate completion coincide with marriage and the realization that I wanted more education.

II. Digging Deeper and Becoming a Father

Graduate school absorbed me intellectually while the birth of a son and daughter were emotional highlights in building family and marriage relationships.

III. First Work Experience

Finally, I left the academic setting and entered the "real" world of R&D at Molecule. Geographically we were removed from family and friends and established new relationships. A third child completed our nuclear family. I adapted to the change in work life and was absorbed in the detail of research projects.

IV. Transitions

I became restless at work and looked for new opportunities. This lead to a short term assignment to Corporate and involvement in project work as distinct from research. My father's death and the difficulty of the circumstances (brain death after resuscitation) had important consequences for my life view and caused some self-searching and introspection. The conflicts and pressures of project work added to my search for the path I wanted to follow.

V. Researcher to Manager

I applied for a supervisory position and got it. The transition included the struggle to resist "doing" research and more toward managing: planning, allocating, explaining . . . Our family grew, my wife went back to work full time.

VI. Increased Responsibility, Maturing Family

A series of changes occurred at work and at home. I received more responsibility, our children left home and married. My wife pursued her own career vigorously.

2) My younger daughter and I went on a backpacking trip with friends in the Colorado Rockies—the area of 14,000 ft peaks. Our goal was to climb Mt. Harvard. The physical climb to above the tree line was difficult and the altitude caused an intense headache. When I awoke the next morning and we continued our climb the experience of beauty of the mountains, the alpine meadows in bloom gave me a high, intensifying my feelings of awe at the great natural beauty, a feeling of accomplishment personally and pleasure that my daughter was with me. The experience intensified my love of the outdoors.

3) My father had a heart attack, was "revived" but remained in a coma for six weeks until death by withholding extraordinary measures based on a diagnosis of "brain death." The waiting with my mother in the hospital, at first with hope, but later with progressive despair was certainly a low. Finally,

participating in the decision. The length of the process and the nature of the circumstances combined to produce probably the deepest low of my life.

4) Father—modeled caring and concern for people along with hard work

Mother—instilled a drive for excellence and intellectual curiosity

Wife—a model of taking charge and getting job done. Also taught me to pay more attention to feelings and intuition

Prof Briggs—modeled behaviors as a researcher and teacher gave me a sense of observing the overall picture, organizing, planning and acting: the model of a research manager

First supervisor: gave me the example of continual questioning of the accepted explanation, the attitude of skepticism and reexamination

S. S. Woodson: example of a team leader getting the job done while paying attention to the people involved, their work, etc.

Manager 6: Superior Performer

1) Adolescent & Teen Years

*Early years memories of nationality discrimination—fighting back

*A high school teacher turns me from a manual arts to college prep program—a pivotal time.

2) The University & an Awakening

*Hard Start at College—almost flunk out—home to decide what important—settle down—strongly improve in studies.—Conflict always in what I want to learn about & where courses are going.

3) Research & Engineering

A happy time—when projects are continued the investigations are exciting—sometimes important. Considerable freedom—the mind is challenged.

4) Management

A change—a new vision on life and on interpersonal relationship, a time for further personal growth—some frustrations—maybe I'd be happier as engineer—The rewards both financial and of job can be good!

5) Beyond Management

Look for future time freedom—would like to maintain intellectual interaction & minimize the B.S. part associated with management. Don't know how yet.

2) At the University—I was engaged at the Bach. level in research on catalytic reactions in gas—I can still remember *very* positive feelings about the work and its importance. Work later won a national award which helped me develop considerable self confidence.

3) My sister and I have always been close even though separated. Her battle with cancer and death a little over two years ago was most painful— Watching her courageous struggle her concern with & for those around her was difficult to say the least.

4) Fr. George Blasic—High School Teacher—pointed me toward college— Recognized I had "something" to offer.

Role model—Mr. Frank Haney—An engineer known to our family, convinced parents to allow me to live at home while doing college work.

Mr. B. Shuster—Prof. at college—special guidance and leadership

Wife & Mother—always encouraging.

What follows is one version of reducing the raw information into an outline that will be easier to work with during the next steps in the identification of themes and code development.

Outline for Manager 1

Question 1
  Infancy
        First—playing

  Glorious Childhood Days
      ⇒ Playing with sisters, friends, classmates
      ⇒ Lost playmates when moved to country
        Out-of-doors—new play arena

The Golden Days
  ⇒ So many fun things to do
  ⇒ At 14 discovered girls—life never the same
    Wedding day

First Marriage
  ⇒ My life really changed
  ⇒ Responsibilities, grad school for oh so long
  ⇒ Grad school trudged on so did relationship
    Sadness followed by despair, medical problems

Single Again
    She left, it was quick, I was numb

Barbara
  ⇒ Came into my life, she was hurting too
  ⇒ Together we learned to live
    PhD, marriage, real job and a family—life can be good

Job, No Career
    Demanding and challenging satisfaction

Question 2
  ⇒ Boss asked me if I would apply for my present job in management
  ⇒ Felt greatly honored—this indicated I was highly thought of as researcher and person
    Since selected my life has become difficult—not an easy job

Question 3
  ⇒ Day I came home to find my first wife had left
    Next day she returned I realized she spent weekend with someone else—remember what she was wearing—how much it hurt

Question 4
  ⇒ Teacher said "You can get the job done, just 'buckle-down'"
  ⇒ Miss Winston—Always expected me to do my best
  ⇒ Father—perfect example of perseverance
  ⇒ My mother—Always loving
    Wife—Always caring

Outline for Manager 2

Question 1
  School years
> Shy, fascinated with things and making them work rather than with people, religion and my obligations to it
Few friends, changing with time

  College
> Opening up—disillusioned with religion
> Joined fraternity, became a socialite
> Wanted to make time pay—into physics adding rigor
> Graduate school—got very specialized
Social life went well, met future wife and married

  Early Molecule Inc.
> Intended college teaching—but ROTC and some luck brought me to Molecule
Made manager less than two years, doing research for 8 more with management as side activity

  Diaspora
> Cutbacks at Molecule—abolished project
> Offered position managing on-line data acquisition
Changed positions several times since, due to project changes, but a couple of times on own

Question 2
> Built complicated nuclear experiment based on theory—took several months, exhilarating to see data come in the way theory said it should, others didn't see it
Affirmation—complex enterprises can work if done right

Question 3
> Learning our project would be terminated—budgetary reasons— same day we completed and successfully tested it
Irony—lack of appeal very disheartening

Question 4
> High school shop teacher taught me to listen to others
> College professor astounded me, admitting "I don't know"—taught emotional honesty

⇒ Grandmother—showed me how to get things done and be positive

⇒ Professor was an inspiring role model

⇒ My wife—artist helped round out my personality

    A couple of instructors showed me a different way of thinking

Outline for Manager 3

Question 1

School Days

⇒ Successful in academics

    Problem—speech impediment, tend to hover in background

Early Career/Marriage

⇒ Left home to seek fortune and fame

⇒ Married—started family

⇒ Successful in first job, left when plant closed

    More grad school

Molecule Career—First Half

⇒ Very successful and satisfying

⇒ Very technically productive

⇒ Appointed supervisor after in job only three years

    Supervisory duties occupied little time—I could continue my technical work

Molecule—Second Half

⇒ Transferred to new organization—went through a few job changes

    Supervisor duties taking more time—Not as satisfying as when I was technically productive

Retirement

⇒ Looking forward to early retirement in about $1\frac{1}{2}$ years

⇒ Returning to purely technical work in another setting

    Children out of school by then

Question 2

⇒ Not a single peak experience, but an activity

⇒ Enjoy teaching—Getting in front of a class, lecturing

    Enjoy explaining complex technical subjects in simple understandable terms—like to see "light bulbs" turn on

Question 3

⇒ Reorganization—3 plus me, managers in one organization lost positions

⇒ Received no explanation, very disheartening, being kicked out of technical area where established reputation and moved to non-supervisory staff job in another organization
Peak experience—making it back to a managerial position

Question 4

⇒ Parents—taught me to be honest and caring with others; encouraged me to pursue my goals
First supervisor—taught me polymer business; taught me to interact with upper management; motivating force behind my technical accomplishments during these years

Outline for Manager 4

Question 1

1. Precollege
   Single, limited expectations

2. College
   ⇒ First step in maturation (personal and professional)
   ⇒ Awareness of my capabilities
   Ideas about career, limited confidence

3. First 10 Years of Work
   ⇒ Blissful happiness with work
   ⇒ Plenty of money, lots of freedom, isolated from reality of budgets by supervisors
   Career already exceeded original dreams

4. Next 10 Years of Work
   ⇒ Growing awareness of abilities
   ⇒ Steered career, overconfident, high expectations
   Felt could contribute more as manager than a researcher

5. Post First 20 Years Till Present
   ⇒ More pragmatic view
   ⇒ Spawned by frustrations in limited resources to do an important job
   ⇒ Overwhelmed by responsibilities
   ⇒ Deep sense of concern for people in my department
   Watch them struggle to do more with less

Question 2
- ⇒ Don't think reached/experienced "peak experience"
- ⇒ Many events fulfilling but still waiting for "peak"
  Only real memories stand out revolve around my family

Question 3
- ⇒ Lowest points revolved around events reminding me of my inherent mortality or many weaknesses
  When diagnosed as having high blood pressure—very hard to accept—demonstrated fragility in life

Question 4

  My Project Leader, then Dept. Manager—profound influence—forced me to expand thinking beyond me; less than a year, whole perspective changed; I admire him for opening my eyes to a whole new career

Outline for Manager 5

Question 1
  I. Establishing the Foundation for Independence
- ⇒ Education for life's work; establishing independence as self-sufficient
  Graduation and marriage, wanted more education

  II. Digging Deeper and Becoming a Father
- ⇒ Grad school absorbing intellectually
  Birth of son and daughter were emotional highlights in building family and marriage relationships

  III. First Work Experience
- ⇒ Left academics, entered "real" world at Molecule, moved
- ⇒ Removed from family/friends, establishing new relationships
- ⇒ Third child—completed our family
  Absorbed in research projects

  IV. Transitions
- ⇒ Restless, looked for new opportunities
- ⇒ Lead to project work as distinct from research
- ⇒ Father's death and difficulty caused self-searching
  Conflicts and pressures at work led to search for path

V. Researcher to Manager
  ⇒ Applied for supervisory job, got it
  ⇒ Transition—struggle to resist "doing" research and more toward managing
  Family grew, wife went back to work

VI. Increased Responsibility, Maturing Family
  ⇒ Changes, more responsibility, children left home and married
  Wife pursued own career

Question 2
  ⇒ Younger daughter and I went backpacking with friends in Rockies
  ⇒ Goal was to climb Mt. Harvard, physical climb to above tree line difficult—intense headache
  ⇒ Awoke next morning and continued climb
  ⇒ Experience of beauty of alpine meadows gave me a high
  ⇒ Feelings of awe at great natural beauty, feeling of accomplishment and pleasure my daughter was with me
  Intensified my love of the outdoors

Question 3
  ⇒ Father had heart attack—revived but in coma for 6 weeks till death by withholding extraordinary measures
  ⇒ Waiting with mother in hospital, first with hope, later with despair was a low
  Participating in decision—length of process and nature produce deepest low of life

Question 4
  ⇒ Father—modeled caring and concern for people with hard work
  ⇒ Mother—instilled drive for excellence and curiosity
  ⇒ Wife—model of taking charge and getting job done—taught me to pay more attention to feelings and intuition
  ⇒ Prof—modeled behavior as researcher and teacher, gave me sense of observing the overall picture, then organizing, planning and acting—model of research manager
  ⇒ First supervisor—example of continual questioning of accepted explanation, attitude of skepticism and reexamination
  S. S. Woodson—a team leader getting the job done while paying attention to people involved, their work

Outline for Manager 6

Question 1
1) Adolescent & Teen Years
   ⇒ Nationality discrimination—fighting back
   High school teacher turns me from manual arts to college

2) University & Awakening
   ⇒ Hard start college—almost flunk out
   ⇒ Home to decide, settle down, improve studies
   Conflict in what I want to learn and courses

3) Research & Engineering
   ⇒ Happy time, projects are exciting
   Freedom—mind is challenged

4) Management
   ⇒ Change—new vision on life and interpersonal relationships
   ⇒ Time for further personal growth
   ⇒ Maybe happier as engineer
   Rewards both financial and of job can be good

5) Beyond Management
   ⇒ Future time freedom
   Maintain intellectual interaction and minimize the B.S. associated with management

Question 2
   ⇒ At the Bach. level—research on catalytic reactions
   ⇒ Very positive feelings about work and its importance
   Work later won national award—helped develop self confidence

Question 3
   ⇒ Sister and I always close, though separated
   ⇒ Her battle with cancer and death, 2 years ago
   ⇒ Most painful—watching her courageous struggle
   Her concern with and for those around her was difficult

Question 4
   ⇒ High school teacher—pointed me to college—saw I had "something"
   ⇒ Engineer known to family convinced parents allow me to live at home while in college

⇒ Prof.—special guidance and leadership
    Wife and mother—always encouraging

Stage II, Step 2: Identifying Themes Within Subsamples

The objective of Step 2 is to sense and articulate potential themes present in a subset of the life stories. At this step, it is easier to use the outlines generated in Step 1. Because the outlines reflect an initial processing of the information (consciously or unconsciously by the researcher), they provide a convenient place to begin perceiving themes. At this stage in the analysis, there is less concern for a detailed, precise description of the theme and more concern for recording any glimmer of themes or patterns among the three life stories in each subset.

The first subset of life stories examined are from Managers 1, 2, and 3, who are from the typical-performing manager sample. During a review of the outlines for Managers 1, 2, and 3, the following themes were identified as possibly characteristic of these three life stories:

⇒ Management as a less attractive role than research; management as a side activity; management not as satisfying as technical work; looking forward to a return to technical work

⇒ Obstacles in life encountered that forced changes in life or activities, such as a plant closing, project/budget cut, reorganization, loss of job, medical problems, or marriage

⇒ Sensitivity to others at work—mention of subordinates and interpersonal relationships

⇒ Fixation at work, having a peak or nadir experience at work (not school)

⇒ External locus of control—others have key role in shaping life and determining fate, focus on friends, experience of loss of respect, attention, love, sense of rejection, and a reactive stance

The second subset of life stories examined is from Managers 4, 5, and 6, who are from the superior-performing manager sample. During a review of the outlines for Managers 4, 5, and 6, the following themes were identified as possibly characteristic of these three life stories:

⇒ Management job is important; resist doing research to spend time managing; management is an opportunity and/or time for further growth

⇒ Obstacles in life encountered that caused introspection or commitment to improve, such as death of loved one or difficulty at school

⇒ Sensitivity to others in family, mention of marriage or divorce and children

⇒ There is a life in addition to work; mention of peak experience with family or death of loved one or experience of own mortality

⇒ Tendency toward self-reflection (mentions feelings, thoughts, attitudes, strengths, weaknesses, a search for meaning, search for right path, recognition of growth opportunities and difficulties)

⇒ Strong career role models

⇒ Personal growth used to enhance life; personal growth seen as key

⇒ Sensitivity to human frailty—explicit description of personal reactions to awareness of how frail life is, emotional growth in response to death or health crisis of another and own mortality

⇒ Role models that taught lessons about helping or considering others

⇒ Reflective about actions of self and others—seeks to understand forces, relative impact and importance of events and circumstance; continually involves self in critical self-assessment to determine strengths and eliminate weaknesses, open to new information that improves self-knowledge and abilities; expresses and acknowledges limitations openly; sober, serious evaluation of events; acknowledge needs, desires, or reliance on others for emotional support or well-being

⇒ Last chapter title—ascendant or present neutral versus descendant or future neutral

⇒ Childhood experiences—isolated, did not experience interpersonal activity (conflict is activity)

Stage II, Step 3: Comparing Themes Across Subsamples

At the point where the researcher feels that he or she has exhausted the potential themes within each subset of life stories, Step 3 begins. First, the researcher examines the lists of themes and looks for themes from each list that may be related. They may appear as polar opposites of a characteristic or may merely seem to involve similar phenomena.

Second, the researcher begins to write or, more accurately, rewrite these potential differentiating themes. Then he or she returns to the original life stories and reads each carefully to see if each story includes the theme, making note of it in the margin for later reference. If a label emerges, the researcher places it as a heading for later consideration as to its appropriateness. For example, in these stories, this step generated the following possible themes from comparison of the outlines. The specific manager's story in which each potentially differentiating theme was found is indicated by his or her identity number in the columns to the right of the theme.

Potentially Differentiating Themes	Superior	Typical
Chapter Headings		
Explicit sequence of time (i.e., first 10 years, second 10 years, etc.)	4	3
Emotion included in heading	5, 6	1
Transitions described of character or affect	5, 6	2
Management Versus Research		
Management as side activity		2, 3
Management not as satisfying as research		3
Promotion based on technical quality		1
Contribute more as manager than as researcher	4	
Life is difficult as manager		1
Management job is very important	4	
Concern for people in department	4	
Questioning: "Maybe I'd be happier as engineer?"	6	
Struggle to resist doing research, keep focus on managing	5	
Management functions of planning, allocating, explaining	5	
Management—a time for further personal growth	6	
Management rewards in job and financial	6	
Mentorship		
Manager protected me	4	
Manager as mentor	4, 5	3
Obstacles to Success Encountered That Forced a Change in Life or Activities		
Plant closing or budget cuts		1, 2
Reorganization—lost job		3
Physical or medical problems	4	1, 3
First marriage		1
Obstacles to Success Encountered That Caused Introspection, Insight, or Commitment to Improve		
Death of loved one	5	
Difficulty at school	6	
Affect and Key Words		
Developing	4	
No, not		1, 2
Limitation, limits	4	
Sadness, despair		1

Potentially Differentiating Themes	Superior	Typical
Disillusioned		2
Challenging		1
Luck		2
Future	4, 6	
Managers or Mentors Helping		
Supervisor protected me from stuff	4	
HS teacher turns me to college	6	
Boss helps	4, 5	3
Future		
Goals: do important work and avoid traps		2
Retirement, return to technical work, go to another setting		3
Future time freedom (minimize BS part of it)	6	
Sensitivity to Others		
Mention of subs at work	4	
Mention of interpersonal relationships at work	6	
Concern with people in department at work	4	
Mention of marriage, divorce, or children (number of sentences)	5 (6)	1 (6), 2 (1), 3 (2)
Marriage, birth of kids as highlight	5	
Peak Experience (Question 2)		
At work		1, 2, 3
Not at work	4, 5, 6	
Influence, reputation, or image enhancement	6	1, 3
Nadir Experience (Question 3)		
Death of loved one, or mention of own brush with death, aware of mortality	4, 5, 6	
Work event		2, 3
Significant Models (Question 4)		
Number of people listed	4 (1), 5 (6), 6 (5)	1 (5), 2 (5), 3 (3)
Teacher: high school or earlier	6	1, 2
Teacher: college	5, 6	2
Parents	5, 6	1, 3
Grandparents		2
Boss	4, 5	3
Focus on technical career		3
Focus on management	4, 5	

Stage II, Step 4: Creating a Code

To begin Step 4, the list of themes identified in the last step is reviewed. The themes showing a distinction between the superior-performing managers (i.e., Managers 4, 5, and 6) and the typical-performing managers (Managers 1, 2, and 3) are then rewritten for maximum clarity and terseness (i.e., parsimony). Can you read any of the six original life stories and clearly see that this theme is present or absent? Is the theme presented with the fewest number of words or concepts possible while maintaining the numerical differentiation? Have you reduced the number of themes as much as possible without losing meaning or confusing phenomena?

The following rewritten themes emerged from the previous list of potential themes. The items present in the list in Step 3 but not in this list were viewed as not clearly differentiating the two subsamples. It was noted, in composing these themes, that Questions 1, 2, and 3 from the life story appeared to reveal differences but that Question 4 did not.

Question 4 may be too strong of a stimulus that overrides any difference of thought patterns between superior- and typical-performing managers. Another possibility is that the culture of this organization encourages the concept of helping others, so that thinking of people who have been role models is a common behavior. Of course, another possibility is that listing or identifying role models and people who have had significant impact on your life is not a characteristic that differentiates people who are superior-and typical-performing managers of scientists and engineers. Regardless of the possibilities, no clear differentiation appears in responses to Question 4. It was dropped from further analysis.

Again, as in Step 3, reading and rereading the original life stories is critical to accuracy and honesty in the process of developing an inductive code. The themes below are presented with the names of the elements of a quality code: label, definition, description of indicators or flags, description of exclusions, and examples. Following the format of the list presented at the end of Chapter 2, the labels of these elements of the code are presented for the reader's ease of recognition. The labels of the elements would not be listed when generating such a thematic code in actual research at this step.

Theme 1

⇒ *Label*—Positive Role Change to Manager

⇒ *Definition*—The person describes the management job and/or the change to a management role as a positive experience.

⇒ *Indicators*—Coded when the person writes, "Management job is important," "Resist doing research to spend time managing," or "Management is opportunity and/or time for further growth."

⇒ *Differentiation*—Managers 1, 2, and 3 did not show this theme; Managers 4, 5, and 6 showed this theme.

Theme 2

⇒ *Label*—Management as Less Attractive Role Than Research

⇒ *Definition*—The person describes the manager's job as not desirable, describes the manager's job as difficult, or describes research as more attractive.

⇒ *Indicators*—Coded when the person writes, "Management as a side activity," "Management not as satisfying as technical," or "Look forward to return to technical work."

⇒ *Exclusion*—The statements should be unqualified (i.e., no "maybe").

⇒ *Differentiation*—Managers 1, 4, 5, and 6 did not show it; Managers 2 and 3 showed it.

Theme 3a

⇒ *Label*—Reactions to Adversity: Problems

⇒ *Definition*- The person identifies obstacles encountered that forced a change in life or activities, such as a plant closing, a project/budget cut, a reorganization and loss of job, medical problems, or marriage.

⇒ *Indicators*—Mentioning any of the above items.

⇒ *Differentiation*—Managers 1, 2, 3, 4, 5, and 6 showed 2, 1, 2, 0, 0, and 0 times mentioning of any such items, respectively.

Theme 3b

⇒ *Label*—Reactions to Adversity: Causing Introspection or Growth

⇒ *Definition*—The person identifies obstacles encountered that caused introspection or building a commitment to improve, such as death of a loved one or difficulty at school.

⇒ *Indicators*—Mentioning any of the above items with the explicit statement that it provoked, stimulated, caused, or led to growth, introspection, or an increased commitment to improve oneself or life.

⇒ *Differentiation*—Managers 1, 2, 3, 4, 5, and 6 showed 0, 0, 0, 0, 1, and 1 time mention of any such items, respectively.

Theme 3, Alternative Conceptualization

⇒ *Label*—Growth-Enhancing Reactions to Adversity

⇒ *Definition*—Theme 3b minus Theme 3a; see above for definitions, flags/ examples, and exclusions.

⇒ *Differentiation*—Managers 1, 2, 3, 4, 5, and 6 would show −2, −1, −2, 0, +1, and +1, respectively.

Theme 4a

⇒ *Label*—Sensitivity to Others at Work

⇒ *Definition*—The person thinks about others in the work organization.

⇒ *Indicators*—Mentioning subordinates or interpersonal relationships.

⇒ *Differentiation*—Managers 1, 2, 3, and 5 showed none. Managers 4 and 6 showed it once each.

Theme 4b

⇒ *Label*—Sensitivity to Others in the Family

⇒ *Definition*—The person thinks about others in his or her family.

⇒ *Indicators*—The number of sentences in which the person mentions a wife/husband or children or mentions marriage or divorce.

⇒ *Exclusion*—Do not code chapter headings.

⇒ *Differentiation*—Managers 1, 2, 3, 4, 5, and 6 showed 5, 1, 2, 0, 5, and 0 sentences, respectively.

Theme 4, Alternative Conceptualization

⇒ *Label*—Sensitivity to the Family Versus Others

⇒ *Definition*—Convert Theme 4b into a presence-or-absence code—was it shown or not from the number of sentences described above? Then calculate this theme as Theme 4b minus Theme 4a; see above for definitions, flags/examples, and exclusions.

⇒ *Differentiation*—Managers 1, 2, 3, 4, 5, and 6 would show −1, −1, −1, +1, +1, and +1, respectively.

Theme 5a

⇒ *Label*—Fixation With Work (as coded from answers to Questions 2 and 3)

⇒ *Definition*—The person thinks about peak and nadir experiences in his or her life from work only.

⇒ *Indicators*—The peak or the nadir experience was a work experience.

⇒ *Exclusion*—Experiences at school (e.g., in graduate school) are not coded.

⇒ *Differentiation*—Managers 1, 2, and 3 showed it. Managers 4, 5, and 6 did not show it.

Theme 5b

⇨ *Label*—Life in Addition to Work (as coded from answers to Questions 2 and 3)

⇨ *Definition*—The person thinks about peak and nadir experiences in his or her life as experiences involving family members, death of loved ones, or his or her own mortality as it threatens these relationships.

⇨ *Indicators*—The peak or the nadir experience involved family members, person mentions the death of a loved one, or person mentions becoming aware of his or her own mortality.

⇨ *Differentiation*—Managers 4, 5, and 6 showed it. Managers 1, 2, and 3 did not show it.

Theme 5, Alternative Conceptualization

⇨ *Label*—A Balanced Life

⇨ *Definition*—Theme 5b minus Theme 5a; see above for definitions, flags/ examples, and exclusions.

⇨ *Differentiation*—Managers 1, 2, 3, 4, 5, and 6 would show −1, −1, −1, +1, +1, and +1, respectively.

Theme 6

⇨ *Label*—Internal Locus of Control

⇨ *Definition*—The person takes decisive, specific action to progress or advance in career or life.

⇨ *Indicators*—Uses the pronoun *I* when expressing ownership of actions, decisions, choices, etc. Self-initiating when seeking challenge, promotional opportunities, or change.

⇨ *Examples*—"I became restless at work and looked for new opportunities." "I applied for a supervisory position."

⇨ *Exclusion*—Do not code if the decision or action is directed by another individual.

⇨ *Differentiation*—Managers 1, 2, 3, 4, 5, and 6 showed 0, 1, 1, 1, 1, and 1. There is a sense that Managers 4, 5, and 6 seem in control of their lives and that the others seem less so. When the original life stories are reread with this theme in mind, it is difficult to assess Manager 6. He seems to be showing it, but many of his statements could be attributed to other forces. Even if he is coded for this theme, there does not appear to be sufficient differentiation to warrant continuing further in the analysis with this theme. If the feeling in the researcher persists that something significant is present, then the researcher should return to the outline and consider alternate flags, examples, and exclusions.

Stage II, Step 5: Determining the Reliability of the Code

Dreyfus (1990) developed a code for a similar but larger subsample of life stories from the same sample of managers, some of whom were the managers in the subsample described here. Her code is different from the one just described in Step 4 and is listed below for comparison. The differences illustrate how different researchers can perceive and conceptualize the same source material.

> *Proactive Attitude Toward Life.* In coding for this category the individual must mention taking action or realization of the ability to take action in situations that reflect agency. Typical life events, such as selecting college major, getting married, starting a family, or getting a first job, are *not* scored. Any of the following qualify:
> ⇒ Takes initiative, directs events, seeks out experiences.
> ⇒ Describes self as agent capable of directing events.
> ⇒ Describes life as a developmental process in which the individual takes an active role.
>
> Examples: "I became restless at work and looked for new opportunities." "Growing awareness of my abilities to take an active role in steering my career as well as the future of the organization." "I applied for a supervisory position and got it." "I left home to seek fame and fortune."

> *Reactive Attitude Toward Life.* In scoring this category the individual describes events as "happening to." If action is taken, it is in response to an event outside of the individual. Any of the following qualify:
> ⇒ Is passive, avoids experiences.
> ⇒ Responds in reaction to events, describes self as acted upon.
> ⇒ Describes life as series of unrelated events over which individual does not have control.
>
> Examples: "And then graduate school for oh so long . . . As the years of grad school trudged on so did the relationship. Sadness crept in, followed by despair, my medical problems, blindness and worse. She left. It was over and final, quickly in six months." "Although I intended to go into college teaching, an ROTC commission and some luck brought me to Molecule, Inc." "I left the organization when the plant closed."

> *Human Frailty.* To score this category there must be mention of the impact that the death of another has had on the individual or the impact of the realization of one's own mortality.

Examples: "My father's death had important consequences for my life view." "The lowest points in my life revolved around events that reminded me of my inherent mortality."

Positive Managerial Role. This category is scored when the individual's specific role of manager is described in a positive way. Any of the following qualify:

⇨ Reference to a positive affective response to the role of manager.

⇨ Mention of the challenge, responsibilities, or rewards of management role as a positive experience.

⇨ Reference to moving beyond previous role and focusing on current role as manager.

⇨ Reference to a developmental or growth producing aspect of the management role.

Examples: "A feeling that I could contribute more as a manager than as an individual researcher." "The transition included the struggle to resist doing research and more toward managing." "Management, a change, a new vision on life and on interpersonal relationship, a time for personal growth."

Negative Managerial Role. In scoring this category the individual does not separate the management role from previous work, and/or expresses a negative reaction to the management role. Any of the following qualify:

⇨ Indications that previous work continues while in the management role.

⇨ Statement that previous work was more satisfying or that returning to previous work would be more satisfying.

⇨ Reference to negative affective response to role as manager.

Examples: "Looking forward to retiring [from management] and returning to purely technical work." "Supervisory duties occupied very little time so I could continue my technical work." "Remained doing research with management as a side activity."

Reflection. To score this category the individual must do one of the following:

⇨ Report actions or realizations that demonstrate an examination of internal thought process or experience.

⇨ Mention a search for meaning, sense making, or soul searching.

⇨ Refer to self-evaluation, introspection, or awareness that goes beyond the self.

Examples: "The conflict and pressures of project work added to my search for the path I wanted to follow." "My father's death and the difficulty of the circumstances had important consequences for my life view and caused some self-searching and introspection." "He *forced* me to expand my thinking beyond my individual career and activities."

Developmental Focus. To score this category the individual must describe events or experiences as having a specific, positive impact that is reported as developmental, growth producing, or critical to further development.

Examples: "[College] the first real step in maturation from both a personal and professional viewpoint." "A high school teacher turns me from a manual arts to college prep program—a pivotal time." "Work later won a national award which helped me develop considerable self-confidence."

Interpersonal Sensitivity. To score this category the individual must include both of the following:

⇒ Express a sense of sharing with or concern about the feelings or emotional experience of another (others).

⇒ Mention a personal reaction to sharing an emotional experience or concern with another (others).

Examples: "A deep sense of concern for the people in my department as I watch them struggle to do more with less." "Watching her courageous struggle, her concern with and for those around her was difficult to say the least." "The waiting with my mother in the hospital, at first with hope, but later with progressive despair was certainly a low." (Dreyfus, 1990, pp. 92-96)

Using percentage agreement scores, Dreyfus (1990) was able to achieve interrater reliability with another colleague of .79 (i.e., the average percentage agreement for the themes), with a range from .75 to 1.00).

Stage III: Steps in Using and Validating a Code

Dreyfus then used the code with all of the remaining managers in the sample (Stage III, Step 1). At this point, she coded the remaining life stories blind to the criterion sample of which each was a part. Once all of the coding was complete and data entered, Dreyfus conducted statistical analyses, as described in Chapter 2 (see Figure 2.3) (Stage III, Step 2). In comparing the superior-and typical-performing managers, she found the following differences or lack of them in the themes in their life stories:

⇒ Proactive attitude toward life was not significant.

⇒ Reactive attitude toward life was significant—typical managers showed more of it than highly effective managers.

⇒ Human frailty was highly significant—highly effective managers showed more of it than typical managers.

⇒ Positive managerial role was not significant.

⇒ Negative managerial role was not significant.

⇒ Reflection was not significant.

⇒ Developmental focus was not significant.

⇒ Interpersonal sensitivity was highly significant—highly effective managers showed more of it than typical managers did.

Having 38% of the themes "validate" (i.e., 3/8) may or may not seem like a sufficient output to justify the tremendous amount of work entailed in developing and validating the thematic code. It is important to note that other methods that Dreyfus (1990) used involved audiotapes of critical incident interviews coded for behavioral competencies (see Chapter 5 for more detail on this method), self-report questionnaires with forced-choice format, self-report card sorts, and self-report questionnaires with rating scales. The array of methods provided important validation of selected abilities or competencies distinguishing superior performance. Establishment of convergent and discriminant validity with the multimethod, multitrait design (Campbell & Fiske, 1959) was made possible because of the addition of thematic coding of the various qualitative methods, particularly the life story and critical incident interview. Dreyfus was able to complement the various quantitative data collection methods with qualitative methods and relate them to each other because of her use of thematic analysis for code development and application. Interpretation of her findings had greater conceptual coherence and meaning as a result of this integration.

Review of Characteristics of a Quality Code

Using material from life stories, this chapter has followed the steps described in Chapter 2 in the development of a thematic code with the data-driven, or inductive, approach. The code was developed to provide maximum distinction between the two categories of the criterion measure—in this example, superior and typical managerial performance. The code developed by Dreyfus (1990) in her original collection and analysis of the life story information was also presented for comparison.

This was not a perfect example of developing a thematic code but was a real one. The ambiguity and possible fuzziness of each step and the resulting description of the emerging themes illustrate the process. Because two codes were described from the same material, it may be helpful to review the list of characteristics considered important for a code to generate insight in qualitative research.

A "good" code (i.e., a code that is usable and has maximum probability of producing high interrater reliability and validity) should have five elements:

1. A label (i.e., a name)
2. A definition of what the theme concerns (i.e., the characteristic or issue constituting the theme)
3. A description of how to know when the theme occurs (i.e., how to "flag" the theme)
4. A description of any qualifications or exclusions to the identification of the theme
5. Examples, both positive and negative, to eliminate possible confusion when looking for the theme

Developing Themes Using the Theory-Driven and Prior-Research-Driven Method and Then Applying the Code

An Example Using a Critical Incident Interview

Using an Existing Code

There are three major reasons for using an existing thematic code with qualitative information. First, the researcher may want to follow his or her own or someone else's earlier research to replicate, extend, or refute prior discoveries. The researcher may also want to use someone else's code as the basis for developing or enhancing a new code. In this situation, the researcher is using the prior-research-driven approach to identify themes and develop a code. Because this method of code development follows a sequence of steps similar to that of the theory-driven approach, the lengthy example and exercise offered in this chapter will reflect both approaches, as the example described in Chapter 2 did.

A second reason for using someone else's code is that a researcher may have clinical, field, or historical documents as raw information and want to use an existing code to establish levels of an independent variable. A third reason is that a researcher may not have the training or confidence to develop his or her own codes and may want to rely on an established code.

Some qualitative researchers have a tendency to develop one code after another. This is often associated with a divergent learning style, restless curiosity, or not having a specific intellectual thrust or theme for one's work. Such a researcher will often do preliminary investigation of a phenomenon and then move on to another phenomenon. If this researcher decides to continue or follow through on initial work, he or she enters into the arena of using thematic codes that have been established.

If the original author of a code or one of his or her associates has developed coder-training materials and, ideally, reliability-testing materials, application of an existing code can be intellectually satisfying. Although learning the other person's code can take time, it takes far more time to develop one's own code. Once the code is learned and interrater or rater-expert reliability is established, the researcher saves considerable time (see Chapter 7 for details of this process).

Someone wanting to investigate a phenomenon in a field or clinical setting or to use available documents in sociology or anthropology may want to use an existing code for one or more variables. Even if he or she wants to develop a thematic code, ascertaining levels of some of the independent variables may require an available code.

An existing code can be learned and applied "as is." When the objective is to replicate, extend, or refute earlier conclusions, a researcher wants to use the existing code *exactly* as it appears in the earlier research. Rater-expert reliability must be determined to confirm that the current researcher is using the same code as the earlier one. Issues and techniques will be discussed in Chapter 7.

There is another way in which a researcher may want to use an existing code: changing it but using it as a basis for a new code (i.e., the prior-research-driven approach to code development). Once the person changes the code or does not establish sufficient interrater reliability with research using the original code, he or she must explain similarity or differences in findings in terms of earlier results. This must be approached delicately and with a great deal of caution. A reviewer could easily critique the work based on a changed code as research using "a different code" and thus not consider it a replication or test of the earlier work. On the other hand, if the variations in the code can be shown to deliver consistent results, a modified code may be considered a comparable code. Similarly, if differences between the original code and current one are shown to be adaptations needed to adjust for different types of raw information, the current research may be considered a replication or test of an earlier work. For example, the original researcher may have studied clinical interviews in which patients' autobiographies were collected on tape. The new researcher may want to extend the investigation to nonpatients and ask people to write an autobiographical essay. The shift from coding interview tapes to coding written essays, not to mention the extension of the study to a new subject population, may require modifying the code.

Availability and Reliability

To use or modify an existing code, the researcher must (a) have access to the code and (b) have access to materials enabling him or her and associates to establish rater-expert or interrater reliability. The issue of attaining interrater reliability with existing codes is relevant only if one is using and applying someone else's code or if one is changing an existing code to a degree not considered conceptually meaningful. Some codes appear in journal articles, often in an appendix, or are available from the researcher on request. Some codes become monographs. To the extent that these monographs also seek to train future researchers, they may become long, heavy books. For example, the code for Kohlberg's stages of moral reasoning is 977 pages long (Colby et al., 1987), and the code for Loevinger's stages of ego development for women and girls is 457 pages (Loevinger, Wessler, & Redmore, 1983). When a code or type of code becomes popular with researchers, such as the codes for the need for achievement, need for affiliation, and need for power, researchers may periodically publish the codes, training materials, and articles to provide guidance. Atkinson provided this service in 1958 with *Motives in Fantasy, Action, and Society,* and 35 years later, Smith, Feld, and Franz (1992) updated and expanded the codes available for use with the Thematic Apperception Test.

As mentioned earlier, establishing reliability with the developers of the original code or earlier researchers is imperative if replication, generalization, or extension of the research is desired. There are various ways to achieve reliability or consistency with the earlier users or developers of a code. They are discussed at length in Chapter 7.

An Example Using a
Critical Incident Interview

To illustrate the development of a code with the prior-research-driven approach and the use of an existing code, the example has been chosen from a longitudinal study of competency development through a person's career. The first two sampling points for this study are the point of entry into an MBA program and graduation from it (Boyatzis, Cowen, & Kolb, 1995; Boyatzis, Leonard, Rhee, & Wheeler, 1996). One of the assessment methods used is a variation of the critical incident interview (CII). Each of the students entering the MBA program at the Weatherhead School of Management at Case Western Reserve University takes a course in which he or she assesses him- or herself and is assessed on 11 knowledge areas known to be important to managers; 22 abilities, of which 20 have been shown to relate to outstanding performance as a manager in multiple organizations; and five value themes (Boyatzis, 1995a, 1995b). The students use this assessment to develop a personalized learning plan as a guide to their desired development during the 2 to 5 years of their MBA program (full-time students take 2 years, part-time students take about 5 years). The students are then assessed at the point of graduation. The research design is to assess them about every 5 years until they retire. The study involves seven cadres of graduating students.

The CII used is a variation on the method first documented by Flanagan (1954). As a form of storytelling, it is a valuable source of qualitative information (Coffey & Atkinson, 1996). It was adapted to assessing a person's competencies by McClelland (1973) and his associates at McBer and Company as the Behavioral Event Interview (Boyatzis, 1982; McClelland, in press; Spencer & Spencer, 1993). The CII, in this context, is a 45-minute to 1-hour interview in which a faculty member asks a student to describe several events in which he or she felt effective at work and several in which he or she felt ineffective. The faculty member is trained in the interview technique to extract the person's story for a number of recent events.

With each event, the student is asked to describe what led up to the situation, who was involved, who did and said what to whom, and the outcome of the event. As the person tells the story of the event, the interviewer is acting more like a journalist than a counselor in attempting to minimize leading cues and get the person to describe actual behaviors and statements made. The desired result should have sufficient detail to enable someone to write a script for a brief play of the event. The interview is audiotaped. Each student is asked for permission to use his or her personal data in the research studies; approximately 89% of each entering class during the years of the studies have granted this permission. Validity of the technique for obtaining descriptions of events and a person's behavior has been reported by Motowidlo et al. (1992) and McClelland (in press).

Stage II, Steps 1 and 2: Refining the Code

The code was developed from prior research on managerial effectiveness. A number of studies comparing superior-performing managers with their less effective counterparts were synthesized into a current model (Boyatzis, 1982; Bray, Campbell, & Grant, 1974; Campbell, Dunnette, Lawler, & Weick, 1970; Howard & Bray, 1988; Kotter, 1982; Luthans et al., 1988; Schroder, 1989; Thorton & Byham, 1982). The research synthesized covered numerous organizations from the public and private sector, in various countries, and managers of both genders.

Using the code developed and validated in my earlier work (Boyatzis, 1982), I reviewed the results from each of the other authors cited above as well as numerous company- and organization-specific research studies of managerial effectiveness. The code for some of the abilities remained fairly consistent with the earlier code, with only minor editorial changes in wording. For some abilities, the name or label was changed, but the code remained the same. For example, *proactivity* from the earlier work was renamed *initiative,* and *perceptual objectivity* was renamed *social objectivity.* In both cases, the indicators and code itself remained unchanged.

For other abilities, research by others resulted in a substantial change in the definition, indicators, and label of the ability. For example, my earlier work described an ability called *stamina and adaptability.* Thorton and Byham (1982) cited numerous studies confirming results for an ability called *behavioral flexibility.* They were building on the earlier work of Bray et al. (1974). The code was constructed around an integration of the concepts of flexibility and adaptability and was named *flexibility.*

The resulting thematic code included competencies or abilities related to effectiveness in management in earlier studies and a few abilities theoretically predicted to relate to managerial effectiveness. The underlying theoretical model of managerial competence looks for those characteristics that lead to or result in outstanding and superior performance as a manager or executive (Boyatzis, 1982, 1995a). The theoretical basis of the earlier work was a foundation for decisions as to the shaping of the current code. Years of research on these abilities in various managerial settings with audiotaped, videotaped, and directly observed data collection had prepared me to consider the themes in the context of the CIIs and videotaped exercises. For any researcher familiar with a form of the "raw information," or data collection technique, Steps 1 and 2 of Stage II are performed at the same time.

For each ability, or competency, the observed behaviors indicating its demonstration are listed as alternate manifestations. That is, if a person demonstrates any of the behavioral indicators listed, the coder can claim that person is demonstrating the "action" level of the ability. Then the coder is asked to infer the person's intent when he or she was demonstrating the behavior. The attempt is to determine "why" the person is demonstrating the behavior. To claim that a person has demonstrated the ability, the coder is asked to determine both one of the behavioral indicators in the code and the intent as described in the definition of the ability. The unit of coding (see Chapter 3 for clarification about units of coding and units of analysis) is the event. In other words, each student can be coded for demonstrating each ability once per event. The only exception is the ability called *self-confidence*. With this ability, the student is coded as showing it across all of the events in the interview. This is required by the condition in the code asking for the person to be consistent in his or her demonstration of the behavioral indicators.

The code used, as originally described in Boyatzis (1995a), is shown below.

1. *Efficiency orientation:* The intent is to perceive input/output relationships and includes the concern for increasing the efficiency of action (i.e., maximizing output per unit of input). This will often appear as a concern for doing something better, whether this comparison is with previous personal performance, others' performance, or a standard of excellence. It is indicated when a person:
   a) Assesses inputs and outputs, or costs and benefits, with the expressed intent of maximizing efficiency (i.e., output/input);
   b) Expresses a concern with doing something better or accomplishing something unique;
   c) Seeks to exceed or outperform a standard of excellence, or goal; or
   d) Uses resources (e.g., time, people, money, etc.) to maximize efficient progress toward goals.

2. *Planning:* The intent is to identify and organize future, or intended actions with a result or direction. It is indicated when a person:
   a) Sets goals or objectives in measurable terms;
   b) Outlines a series of actions, at least three actions, toward achieving a goal (the link to the goal must be clear, if not explicit) or overcoming a stated obstacle to achievement of a goal;
   c) Organizes materials or activities to accomplish a task or reach a goal;

d) Takes calculated risks, evident in assessing and moderating risks in a situation prior to taking action; or

e) Anticipates obstacles to a course of action and describes what to do to overcome them, should they occur (i.e., contingency planning).

3. *Initiative:* The intent is to take action to accomplish something, and to take this action prior to being asked or forced or provoked into it. A person displaying initiative is clearly identified as the initiator of actions in a situation. It is indicated when a person:

a) Takes action first, not reacting to or being forced by events (e.g., he/she seizes opportunities);

b) Takes action by seeking information in a non-traditional or unusual way (e.g., utilizes a wide variety of sources of information not typically used); or

c) Takes action different than anyone else or the expectations of others.

4. *Attention to detail:* The intent is to seek order and predictability by reducing uncertainty. This is often enacted by a person giving careful consideration prior to and taking actions (e.g., making sure that your shoes are shined, as well as your clothes pressed prior to a presentation). It is indicated when a person:

a) Shows consistent attention to detail (e.g., double checks information or accuracy of own or others' work, summarizes group discussion, etc.); or

b) Keeps records diligently.

5. *Self-control:* The intent is to inhibit personal needs or desires for the benefit of organizational, family, or group needs. Although it is often not visible (i.e., if a person has self-control you cannot easily see them controlling himself/herself), it is indicated when a person:

a) Remains calm in stressful settings (e.g., when being attacked);

b) Explicitly inhibits aggressive outbursts or impulsive behavior that may hurt others or hurt progress toward goals; or

c) Explicitly denies a personal impulse, need, or desire (i.e., makes a personal sacrifice) for the good of an organizational or group need.

6. *Flexibility:* The intent is to adapt to changing circumstances, or alter one's behavior to better fit the situation. It is often associated with a tolerance for ambiguity and uncertainty. It is indicated when a person:

a) Changes a plan, behavior, or approach to one that is more appropriate in response to a major change in a situation or changing circumstances; or

b) Changes a plan, behavior, or approach to a situation to one perceived to be more appropriate when the desired impact is not occurring.

7. *Empathy:* The intent is to understand others. It is indicated when a person:
   a) Understands the strengths and limitations of others;
   b) Understands the reasons for others' behavior (i.e., knows what motivates or demotivates specific other individuals);
   c) Accurately reads, or interprets the moods, feelings, or nonverbal behavior of others; or
   d) Listens to others by asking questions and waiting for their reply, or taking the time to allow another person to explain or describe something at his/her own pace and manner.

8. *Persuasiveness:* The intent is to convince another person, or persons of the merits of, or to adopt, an attitude, opinion, or position (i.e., getting others to do or think what you want them to do or think). It is indicated when a person:
   a) Gives directions or orders based on the rules, procedures, government regulations, authority of their position in the organization, or personal authority without soliciting the input of others;
   b) Explicitly expresses a need or desire to persuade others;
   c) Attempts to convince others by appealing to their interests (i.e., pointing out what each will gain personally);
   d) Attempts to convince others by anticipating how people will react to an argument, appeal, or situation and develops the communication to their level of understanding or emotional condition at that time;
   e) Uses questions or other techniques explicitly intended to result in the audience feeling and accepting ownership of the ideas, projects, or activities; or
   f) Explicitly expresses concern with his/her image and reputation, the image or reputation of his/her organization, or its products and services.

9. *Networking:* The intent is to build relationships, whether they are one-to-one relations, a coalition, an alliance, or a complex set of relationships among a group of people. It is indicated when a person:
   a) Acts to build a relationship with someone that might be useful in the present or in the future to accomplish a task;
   b) Maintains personal relationships that are, or might be work-related; or
   c) Uses a network of informal relationships to get things done.

10. *Negotiating:* The intent is to stimulate individuals or groups toward resolution of a conflict. This ability may be demonstrated in situations in which

the person is one of the parties in the conflict or merely a third party. It is indicated when a person:

a) Involves all parties in openly discussing the conflict with the intent of resolving the conflict;

b) Identifies areas of mutual interest or benefit, often an objective to which all parties can aspire; or

c) Determines the concerns, or positions of each of the parties and communicates them to all involved as an initial step toward open discussion of the conflict.

11. *Self-confidence:* The intent is to consistently display decisiveness or presence. It is indicated when a person:

a) Consistently presents himself/herself, verbally or nonverbally, in an assured, forceful, impressive, and unhesitating manner; or

b) Consistently expresses the belief that he/she is among the best and most capable for a job, and likely to succeed.

12. *Group management:* The intent is to stimulate members of a group to work together effectively. It is indicated when a person:

a) Creates symbols of group identity, pride, trust, or team effort;

b) Acts to promote commitment to a team, task, or shared goal through friendly, personal contact;

c) Involves all parties concerned in openly resolving conflicts within the group as a vehicle toward collaboration among the group members;

d) Allows the group to take responsibility for certain task accomplishments and does not assume personal responsibility for them; or

e) Explicitly communicates to others the need for cooperation or teamwork within the group.

13. *Developing others:* The intent is to stimulate someone to develop his/her abilities or improve their performance toward an objective. It is indicated when a person:

a) Gives someone performance feedback to be used in improving or maintaining effective performance;

b) Provides others with information, tools, other resources, or opportunities to help them get their job done or to improve their abilities (e.g., giving a promotion as part of their development);

c) Invites others to discuss performance problems with the explicit purpose of improving their performance; or

d) Explicitly tells another that he/she can accomplish an objective and provides encouragement and support.

14. *Systems thinking:* The intent is to order multiple causal events. It is indicated when a person:
   a) Describes multiple causal events (i.e., multiple cause and effect relationships) in terms of a series, or plan of action and events or flow diagram; or
   b) Establishes priorities among a list of at least three alternate actions reflecting a concept of multiple causality (i.e., A should be done first because it leads to B, which leads to C and we want C to occur).

15. *Pattern recognition:* The intent is to identify a pattern in an assortment of information, unorganized, or seemingly random data. It is indicated when a person:
   a) Identifies a pattern in events or information not used by others and uses the pattern to explain or interpret the events or information;
   b) Reduces large amounts of information through the use of a concept not previously applied to this situation or information;
   c) Sees similarities of a new situation to aspects of past situations of a different type; or
   d) Uses metaphors or analogies to explain events or information (this should be more than a figure of speech or single phrase).

16. *Social objectivity:* The intent is to perceive another person's beliefs, emotions, and perspectives, particularly when they are different from the observer's own beliefs, emotions, and perspectives. It is indicated when a person:
   a) Perceives multiple perspectives, or views, of the same situation or issue;
   b) Sees merits of differing perspectives, especially when they are different than his/her own; or
   c) Describes another person's thoughts, feelings, or values as unique to the individual in the context of others claiming or making stereotypical generalizations about the person because of a group, or category of individuals to which he/she belongs. (Boyatzis, 1995a, pp. 82-90)

This code includes 16 of the 20 abilities, or competencies, assessed in the course and the longitudinal studies. The code is used to assess abilities demonstrated during the audiotaped CII and videotaped exercises, such as the Group Discussion Exercise and Presentation Exercise. (See Boyatzis, 1995a, for a detailed description of the course and Boyatzis, Baker, Leonard, Rhee, & Thompson, 1995, for a description of the videotaped exercises used in the studies.)

Stage II, Step 3: Determining Reliability, and Stage III, Step 1: Applying the Code to the Entire Sample

All prospective coders are faculty or advanced doctoral students who engage in a doctoral seminar on thematic analysis, 1 week of training in the course methods, 2 to 3 weeks of coder training using a computer-based coder-training system and tutorials. Following the training, each person must pass a coder reliability test demonstrating at least 70% reliability with experts on the 14 most frequently coded of the 18 abilities possibly assessed with the CII in the course. For this example, we are using only 16 of them. The experts who determined the expert coding for the coder test were three faculty members or researchers who had developed these codes (Boyatzis, 1982) and others who had used codes in criterion-referenced managerial competency studies (Dreyfus, 1990; Leonard et al., 1995).

In the most recent research studies reported by Boyatzis et al. (1996), two of three coders independently coded each audiotaped interview. The reliability of each of the pairs on the original coding of the 16 abilities averaged 88%, 89%, and 89%, with medians of 88%, 88%, and 91% and ranges of 61% to 100%, 81% to 97%, and 66% to 97%, respectively. The pair compared their assessments and reconciled differences with a third coder. By the time the two coders had discussed differences with each other and a fourth person who was a trained coder, they had achieved 100% agreement. Of the 18 abilities that can be coded from the CII, two were dropped from being coded with the CII from 1994 onward.

The Example and Exercise:
Mary Simpson, an Entering MBA Student

Mary Simpson was 34 years old when she entered the part-time MBA program. She had graduated with a degree in engineering and gravitated toward computer sciences during her undergraduate years. She got a job in the systems programming unit of a consumer products division of a large industrial company. Over the years, her performance was noticed, and she was given various promotions, eventually entering supervisory and management positions in information systems at the company. Mary's decision to enter the MBA program was driven by a desire to learn how to manage and prepare herself for general management by learning aspects of management other than information systems.

At the beginning of the interview, the faculty member explains·the objective of the interview and why it is being audiotaped. The faculty member then engages the student in 10 to 15 minutes of discussion of the student's recent career history. Because it is used to establish rapport and familiarity but is not useful in observing behavioral patterns, this segment of the interview is not taped. The following interview covered three incidents.

Those segments of the interview thought to illustrate one of the abilities included in the code appear in **bold italics**. Following each highlighted segment is the word *Note* followed by a number. Following the transcript of the entire interview, each of the notes is listed, naming which ability was coded in the corresponding segment. A brief explanation as to why it was coded is provided.

If you wish to use this as an exercise, use the code previously described and see if you can identify which of the competencies is being demonstrated each time you encounter a highlighted section. It is important to note that at times a highlighted section may illustrate the demonstration of more than one competency.

Incident 1

> *Faculty:* Okay, so this is an effective one?
>
> *Simpson:* The most recent one I can recall that was very effective for me and successful was a migration from a current computer system to a new architecture. The current system that was in place at the time had about 120 users on the system, and we were running an entire integrated business system for all business functions throughout the company. My responsibility and challenge was to migrate that whole computer system to another computer system, a new type of architecture without any glitches, and that meant that it started on Friday night, by Monday morning the business was up and running because we're not a seven-day business. We're a six-day business, and the seventh day is a resting day for us. That's just company policy. So, not to say that won't change, but in this case I had two days to implement the procedure, and the original plan started a year prior to the implementation which happened to be almost, I would say, eight to ten months ago. And the whole thing started by going to a training class in Chicago by a computer company, which in this case, was TCC.
>
> *Faculty:* Let me stop you right there. Who went to the training class?

Simpson: I did personally. Only myself, because it was my project, and I report directly to the V.P. of Finance, so he is not only the chief financial officer, but the chief information officer, and *this was my turning point, so to say, at that time I was a supervisor of computer operations, and if I proved to be successful, I'm sure that this was the turning point for me to get a promotion because I'd been with the company for eight years, and had been working towards this.[Note 1] So I went to this training class and spent a week learning about the new system, and the transition that would need to be taking place, and there were other managers and operations people from all over the country that, you know, they pay for the class as well to come in. And not only do you learn about it, but you interact with each other and ask each other what types of businesses you have so that you might get a flavor for the real world versus what a vendor tells you. Because it isn't always the same. So that proved to be very valuable, probably more valuable than the class itself. [Note 2]* And I brought back a notebook. *I created a binder, and I tabbed it by, really by category, and what needed to be done in terms of the actual devices themselves that had to be switched, so you had parts of the system that were unusable, and you had to get new equipment to replace that.[Note 3]* So you have before and after kind of situation, so I had hardware. *I had software, I had operations, and different phases that had to take place. After that binder was created, I went and scheduled visits for other businesses that had already made the transition. I made three such visits to different companies in Ohio and talked about how they did it. And even though they might be a little bit smaller, a little bit bigger, it still is the same type of architecture, so it was the same situation. And those proved to be very valuable to me to use because I learned on their mistakes, and made sure that we didn't have the same problems that they did.[Note 4]* The next thing I had to do was create a proposal on the cost of all this. *What it was going to cost from the actual purchase to the implementation, which I laid out in a document in capital appropriation letters of a corporate policy-type of thing where you have to account for that piece of equipment that's going to be capitalized, and will have a scheduled depreciation against it. So that was presented, and immediate management signed it, and then it had to go to corporate, which is, we're a division of _____, and then it went to their financial officers, and then the head of the corporate MIS scheduled a meeting to come out and visit with me to make sure that, did I indeed know what I was talking about, I was putting in a half-a-million-dollar system.[Note 5]* Did I dot my i's, cross my t's? Is this really the right system for where we're going? So he came out, and he met along with my boss just to make sure, and they went ahead and approved it, and we scheduled the equipment to come in, and then I started preparing all the background things that I could accomplish in terms of, what can I do? *I had about four or five different vendors that had to be scheduled to accommodate one another all at one time, because you can't do one thing without another. So I had to set up time tables, and how this whole process would theoretically happen in that scheduled time, and so we all met on several different occasions. I had meetings, and I invited them all, and we had a round-table together to discuss, was this feasible to them, is it something that is going to be understandable, and did they all agree to that situation. And they felt that they did, so we waited until the equipment came in, and we went ahead and had it installed. What I did was, rather than get rid of the old one and put the new one in, I had them running parallel, which means that, if something should happen, I could always revert back to the other system. Now, there still would have been some hardware problems, because I had, say, all the terminals hooked up to this one, but I still had a copy of all the software over here. And if push came to shove, it would have been a matter of just disconnecting the terminals, and plugging them there. So I ran parallel for about thirty days, and you know pretty much up front when an installation is good or bad by the first or second day, because things start going askew right away.[Note 6]* So they all came in, it was tested, we had one minor glitch, like on the day that it was installed, and the group came back, and fixed it, and it was installed, and by Monday we were up and running, and we had no down time, literally, at all. And in thirty days we got rid of the other machine, and we did all of the follow-up work, and then we went back and said, what did we do well, what did we not do so well, and what would we do differently?

Faculty: Who do you mean by "we"?

Simpson: Well, I was the project leader, and I have a staff that works for me, and they helped, obviously I couldn't do this all myself, I had a staff of operations people, and the vendors, I mean, they wanted to know their performance, and how they did, because it's really going to help them down the road in how they can help their customers when you're putting in that five-year system. And it was a very successful install. And in doing that, a lot of people came to my shop then, and asked us how we did, and it was kind of like passing the buck, and helping out a colleague.

Faculty: Okay. Let's go back. I need to get some more details.

Simpson: Okay.

Faculty: That was great. You talked about the creation of the binder, category by category, and what needed to be done. Tell me how you created the binder.

Simpson: Do you mean how my thought process was? Why I decided to do that? *Because the project was so big I really in my experience in the last several years of working for this man I've learned that you can't tackle something that big all at once, and when you're justifying something to someone it's much easier to put it in smaller pieces, and it is for me. I've learned that's where ineffectively I went astray, but effectively, I just chose, they're just logical choices.[Note 7]* In computers there's users, there's hardware, there's software, and communication, which is another piece of it. Operationally, which means, after you do the hardware, which is the install portion of it, and then the software, which is the application portion of it, the communications, which is, we have remote facilities in California, Canada, Missouri, and Chicago. *Without the communications they can't get to it, so it's kind of like a puzzle, and it kind of unfolds, and if you do one piece at a time, you see it coming together, and you can't do one without the other. You can't install software without the hardware. You can't use the communications without either one of those [Note 8], and operationally, the procedure is to be able to take those steps that will allow you to operate the machine at that point, and then testing, which is testing it to make sure, let's say I'd run a program in every application to make sure that all your business functions were taken care of. I did that just for my own protection, you know, to make sure, did I do everything, did I really think of everything? [Note 9]* And it was just easier to go to, if I had a question, I'd think, Oh, that's hardware, then I'd go there. I had to consolidate it all for me, cause it was too big of a project.

Faculty: Okay. How did you go about the different phases? You talked about there were different phases, and I had to schedule visits with other . . . well, let's talk about the different phases first. Do you remember what you said about that?

Simpson: The different phases of the project? *Well, to me the different phases were just as I presented it was: Phase one was identifying your need—why do you need a new computer, well, you're running out of gas, and you need to get a bigger system to accommodate your business. The next phase was identifying the computer that you need, getting the right one. And so you go visit people and ask them, well how big is your business? And what kind of business do you have, what's your transaction volume, being able to ask the right questions to be able to define is that the correct piece of hardware or are we really, what's the performance level between what you have and where you're going, is it one time, two times? And that's a phase. Then, the next phase is identifying the components out of that that you need, and then it's purchasing it, or justifying it, purchasing it, implementing it.[Note 10]*

Faculty: Okay. Let's talk about the visits. You scheduled visits with other companies who had already done this. How did you go about doing that?

Simpson: Well, obviously, the vendor that we're buying the computer from has sold it to other people. And I just asked, is there any businesses that you sold this to—I usually don't buy anything—I don't like to be the first one on the block because it usually is trouble when you do that. So what I did is I asked, is there anyone that installed this system yet, and they said, yes, and they gave me several names. *And I said, well, would you mind if I would call the MIS director or whoever it was, and they said, well, why don't you let me call them first and ask them if they would mind. And so my sales rep called them and they said not, and then I made the contact—we scheduled a visit. And I made some really nice business partnerships, we keep in touch now, and we see each other. But you just call them up, and, you know, and say, I'm _____ of the _____ Company, and I'm responsible for installing, and implementing the new system, and I was wondering if I could come and visit with you for a day, or have lunch, or discuss things over several hours.[Note 11]* They were all more than happy to comply, which was really refreshing, and most of the directors, obviously, didn't have the answers because their technical people under them were the ones that installed it, but they could talk about the phase project, and how they went about the whole approval process, and how they justified it to management. And so I kind of felt that I was, like on two levels, which was really quite nice. And that's all there was to it, just calling them.

Faculty: Okay. Is there any particular one that stands out, one particular visit?

Simpson: Yeah.

Faculty: Will you tell me about it?

Simpson: Well, this gentleman is a V.P. of MIS, and their corporate headquarters is in Maine, and his MIS office is in Middletown [disguised place], which is where I live. *And he was a very, he was an older man, he'd been in the business over twenty years, so he was very knowledgeable. And I haven't found too many people that have that kind of responsibility that are willing to share with someone of my experience in years. He sat down, he was a gentleman, he was a very low-key, soft-spoken man. At the same time, his shop was running around him. It was a glass enclosure, and there were people everywhere, and they were constantly interrupting, and they were constantly phoning, and he never once rippled, I mean, he was very people oriented, but yet he answered their questions, and he would always be courteous to me, and I understood the situation, so I didn't mind it when we were interrupted, but he allowed his people to run this project, and he didn't have a really large ego, and he gave them most of the credit.[Note 12]*

Faculty: How did you know that?

Simpson: Well, that's my impression of him, and . . .

Faculty: What gave you that impression?

Simpson: Because of the fact that he always talked about what "they" did, he never used the word *I* or *me,* he'd always use a team concept, a *we* or *us* or *Bill,* who was the project leader. And then he turned it over to Bill, you know, and Bill was in there with us, and he let Bill talk. And he just didn't take any of the glory away from what the guy did, even though he might have done it all, you know, you just felt that they were a team, they were a group. And I like that, and that's one of the things that I would like to strive for, cause it's just so easy to do something like this and take all the credit for it, but, you know, it is a team effort, and I am unlike that, more, I don't know if it's his experience or where he's come from, but that really stuck out in my mind.

Faculty: Okay. Let's go on to the, you said, you created the cost proposal? Tell me how you did that.

Simpson: Well, based upon the different vendors that I had, and different categories I had, which is hardware and software, communications, miscel- laneous items, I sat down and wrote a memo and outlined those categories, and then, well, I wrote an introductory paragraph stating what the whole project was, and what the outcome was supposed to be, and why we were doing it. And then, I said, these are the following issues, and costs that are part of this whole proposal, which is, you know, I outlined it, and then showed a detailed, one item by line item cost, with everything, and then subtotaled it, less discount, and adjustments, and gave them a bottom-line number. I just took proposals from all these vendors that I had for all the various parts that, parts pieces that we had, and brought it all together and then did an outline, and just put it in a memo format, and then had a cover sheet, which is our corporate layout, and then you just, it's like a summary sheet, and then it has all the signatures on it that, you have your controller, and your general manager for that division, and the project manager, and it goes through all the levels, and depending on what the dollar cost is, that person has to sign off on it, in this case it had to go all the way to the board of directors because it was a high item.[Note 13]

Faculty: Okay. And you said you prepared background things to accomplish, and you had to schedule vendors, and create a timetable. How did you go about doing that?

Simpson: When, once you knew that it was approved and you had meetings to bring all these people together, you wanted to know how much you could get done up front without the company being down, so you wanted to get as much done as you could possibly do—what can I do, outside of bringing the company down, and then what do I have to do, what can I only do after I bring the company down. So I knew I had two days of nobody on the system, what could I do to give me more of a time to test and to make sure everything was okay. So I identified those with help of experience, and the people that have done it, and the vendors that came in, and then I labeled, what can we do before we bring the system down, and then, what do we have to wait for, and that's how we proceeded. We had a checklist that, you know, one, two, three, four, and then capital one, capital two, was after the system was down, and just, it was very, it was like a cookbook set of instructions, and it just, that made all the difference in the world. All that planning, and all the organization showed me, which I really hadn't experienced up to that point, how successful something like that could be.[Note 14]

Faculty: Great. What was the final outcome?

Simpson: The final outcome was, the system was installed successfully, it ran, there was no down time, it's still running, and I got promoted.

Faculty: Anything else you want to add?

Simpson: Just that I think this is a case where my boss was good enough to give me the opportunity to try, and he could have stepped in at any point and said, no, do it this way, try this, don't do that, I want to see it every week. He never butted in, he never once criticized the way I handled it, he asked me if I would mind copying him on the final outcome before I send it to corporate, and I said that that was fine. I wanted him to, I wanted some feedback, one because I was a little nervous sending that big of a proposal without approval, and we reviewed it, and we cleaned it up a little bit, but I think for me that this is a case where I got the opportunity to give something a try. I mean, I've gone through years of experience before this point, but this was, he was giving me the opportunity to grow, and to learn, and I would hope to do that for somebody someday, so that's . . .

Incident 2

Faculty: That's exactly what I was looking for, to a tee. You want to come up with another one? An ineffective one?

Simpson: I think to preface an ineffective one for me, I'm a person that, I need time to think about something. I'm not fast at anything. I don't read fast. I don't think fast, and it's not that I don't want to, I just, I don't seem to be able to, and often times when people, in dealing with people at work, I manage a few people, I seem to be ineffective in showing the people the way I really want them to see an issue. I don't seem to be able to communicate to them the value of what they do, versus, I'm more like, let me show you, rather than giving them an opportunity and being patient. I'm kind of a, for me, I'm very ineffective with doing something very quickly, and when you're dealing with another human being, or it's a very heated situation, I tend to react versus sitting back. And that's kind of a contradiction of itself. I react, but it's not really the way that I am.

Faculty: Can you give me an example of that?

Simpson: I'll tell you a situation that I handled very, very poorly.

Faculty: Okay.

Simpson: Is, I went on vacation, and while I was away, they shut the system down for a whole day, and I felt that the people that were handling it. Fine, I mean, I gave them the responsibility. I gave them the opportunity to handle the situation, and I wasn't going to butt in. They had my phone number. The system did not come back up correctly, and the operator was really very young and inexperienced. He called my house and left a message on my recording machine, and said that the system came up, but he said something technical, and I thought, well, it'll be okay, the programmer comes in at six a.m., he'll fix it. Well, here what he was saying was the power came up, but the system did not come up, he just didn't use the right language. So the system was down, he went home, the programmer-analyst came in, and he handled the situation versus letting the senior operations person handle it, and he did not get the system up for the whole day. I had a business out of service until ten-thirty that night. He took it upon himself to send the operator home when it was the operator's responsibility, and because he didn't understand operations, he called the wrong things, which subsequently left the system in a longer down time than it should have. *I came in on Tuesday, and people have a tendency to greet you in the parking lot, bring you, I mean, you don't even get to put your briefcase down or get a cup of coffee, and people are jumping on you, and you just had a vacation, you're trying to be calm, and they're saying the system was down. And my boss was in Maine, I mean, he was gone, so there was nobody there. Right away, started getting a conflict, you know, and I listened, and I didn't say anything, then I went in and the programmer-analyst said that he, he told me all the things he did, and I got piqued at him. I was upset because right away, instead of looking at it, like he did what he thought was best, and he handled the situation as best he could, I turned it into a situation where it was, thanks a lot but don't do it again.[Note 15]* So I was . . .

Faculty: What did you have to say to him? Do you remember?

Simpson: I was talking to him and the more I was talking to him I was getting more curt and more, and see, that's where I have this real ability to come off that way, and I don't mean to be that way. So my personality kind of like started to really, I was pouncing on him. And here this guy was doing the best that he could do, and he thought he was doing the right thing, and I was giving him heck for trying. And I said to him, something like, I really appreciate, thanks a lot, I really appreciate it, and the way I said it was really terrible. And I walked away, and I thought, gee, _____, you know, and I felt really bad about it, so that was really an ineffective type of interaction with an employee, and my boss came back to me and told me about it.

Faculty: Told you what?

Simpson: How I handled that situation. Because this employee went out to lunch with my boss, and, you know, was saying, do you understand _____? I don't really understand her that well, I don't quite understand her moods, you know, how she is, and the way she is, and I tend to be more afraid to be wrong type of thing, you know, so I'm quiet, which is part of not wanting to do anything quickly. So you can't, you know, those are personality traits that, you know, I have to deal with as a manager, but at the same time I'm dealing with other people's lives. And it's good that I recognize it, but it makes me very ineffective, because I should have been praising him for doing the best that he could, and tried to be constructive in a way where I didn't take away his self-worth. So . . .

Faculty: What happened next?

Simpson: After that?

Faculty: You talked to the program-analyst and then what happened?

Simpson: I took the operations person aside and asked him, why did he not take the responsibility that was so clearly his, and he said that he felt that the programmer-analyst was handling it and that he just didn't want to take the responsibility, and, you know, I reminded him that that's what he's being paid for, and that's why he was hired, and we sent him to many training classes just for operations, and that this is a clear situation of youth and inexperience versus, I mean, the programmer-analyst is fifteen years older than him, and a few years more in the workplace.[Note 16] And it's a male situation as well. I mean, there's now ego involved, and I, a woman, trying to make my way into the business world, and often times I beat my head up against the wall. And that's not always true, it doesn't always happen, but when it does, I don't handle it well, so I'm very ineffective emotionally. So my ineffectiveness might be my emotions that are the case, and I'm still uncertain, but I think that's probably the one thing that comes to my mind about how I am ineffective as a manager with people.[Note 17] Because when something, you know, if it's everyday kind of thing, I'm fine, but if it's a crisis, like I've been away, like I went away that weekend, then two weeks ago it happened again.

Faculty: The system went down?

Simpson: The system went down. The same problem, a different disk, and it happened fine because the operator talked to me on the phone, and I worked with him for twenty-four hours then. And then last weekend I was away, and I came back, and one of my operators quit. Put in their notice on Monday, and left on Friday. Had nothing to do with me, luckily, but, I mean, it's quite a track record in a very short period of time.

Faculty: Let's go back to your supervisor. You said that the program-analyst had had lunch with your supervisor, and asked questions. Tell me about the interaction you and your supervisor had after that conversation.

Simpson: Well, he called me in, and it was, he didn't call me in intentionally for that, which, again, he's very good at that type of thing, and he didn't focus in, like, I had lunch with _____ and he told me this. We were talking about issues, and we meet on a weekly basis, and he said to me first of all, _____ by rights, the programmer-analyst really shouldn't go out with a V.P. in Finance. I mean, it would be like if I went out with the president of the company, and talked about the V.P. of Finance to him, and he would come in to the V.P. of Finance, and say, you know _____'s not real happy about certain things, you know. And so not wanting to let me know, he said, I want you to know that I've gone to lunch with _____, he calls me up, and I can't say "no," how do you feel about it? And I said, well, I said, it's an open-door-policy, and you're more than welcome to, I said, however, it does make me ineffective at times because you are my boss, and ultimately, you are the chief information officer, and he feels that you can over-ride me in situations, and it kind of makes me look a little ineffective in the whole situation, which is the right word, because that's what happens. He said, well, he said, I don't really want to stop, he said, because he's a valuable employee, but I don't want you to think that we're sitting there talking about you, either. I said, well, I'm not really worried about that. I said, if you were I'd think you were really a poor manager, and I said, you know, if that's what you value doing then that's good, but. Then, I said what did he talk about that's so important? Then he felt that he didn't have a problem telling me what they talked about, and he said, to be honest with you, he said, he talked to me about details that I really don't want to know about, but I'm really nice. He said that, he said, he doesn't quite understand you. And I said, well, what is there to understand? I said, most of us don't understand our bosses, you know, one day they're this way, the next day they're that way. I think you're going to make a decision this way, you change your mind. And he said, well, he just doesn't understand why you want to be called when there's a crisis, when they can handle it, and, two, he wants to be your number two person. And I looked at him, and I said, well, you know, I know he does, but, you know, clearly it wasn't his responsibility, and when it comes right down to it, yes, I guess he is the number two person, because he knows the most and that's who you want to rely on. So, but I don't understand why you have to come and tell me that, you know. Why are you pleading his case for me? I said, how would you feel if I went into the president's office, and he came in, and he said, I wouldn't like it. He said, but you can do that if you want. But I wouldn't do that to you, you know, I just wouldn't. So I think it's a mind-set in my mind on what's right, so maybe I take that and utilize that in an incorrect fashion, as if there's no loyalty or, it's not that he's after my job because he's a programmer-analyst and he's not interested in becoming, like a manager or a leader in information systems, he just wants to be an analyst or a designer of software. So it's not really that.

Faculty: What was the final outcome?

Simpson: The outcome was that, personally, I assessed the whole situation and vowed to be calmer under a crisis, and to try to allow people to be human, and to let them probably have a little more freedom than I was willing to give at that time. I mean, I really thought about it a lot, and I felt badly how I treated him, which was wrong. Even though I felt that the situation wasn't handled correctly, the system went back up, and my boss and I talked about it, and my programmer-analyst and I talked about it. Everybody talked about it, so we got it out in the open, and I feel that that's the most important thing, because everyone said what was on their mind.

Faculty: The conversation you had with the program-analyst, do you remember that?

Simpson: After?

Faculty: Yes.

Simpson: I tried not to divulge the fact that he and _____ had went to lunch, and I knew the whole conversation. I did not discuss that, however, I did ask him if he was happy, you know, just in the course of the conversation, we have lunch every two weeks together to go over business issues. He was quiet and very hesitant, and, you know, he came out and said the same things that _____ had told me that he said. And you know, I told him, I apologized the way I handled it. I said that I did not handle it correctly, and, finally, he had to understand where I was coming from, which was, I am ultimately responsible, and he was taking that responsibility away from me by making the decision to say, I didn't call you because I didn't feel that we needed to, we were handling it. So the outcome was that he put his cards on the table, and I put mine on the table, and he seemed to feel a lot better about it, and the resolve is that we have better communication with each other now. The last several weeks has probably been the easiest time that we've had.[Notes 18 and 19]

Faculty: You said he seemed to feel better? How do you know?

Simpson: Just by his attitude. He's been more relaxed. He'll come over and joke and just talk outside of business, you know, he'll just come over, and, how-'ya-doing kind of thing. Before it was mostly all business.

Faculty: Okay. Anything else you want to add?

Simpson: To that?

Faculty: Yeah.

Simpson: No.

Incident 3

Faculty: We have time for one more. Let's end on a positive note.

Simpson: Yeah. Effectiveness . . . I think I need . . .

Faculty: So this is going to be an effective one?

Simpson: This is effective. This project started four years ago, and we have an outside software group that does all of our major programming, business applications, and I had the opportunity to start a project called EDI, or Electronic Data Interchange, which is a box-to-box order entry, meaning, if a company has an order they now will transmit it to a third party network which is called GE or Order-Net or McDonald-Douglas, and it's like a mailbox and then you go out and pick up your mail and bring it in. And it goes into your computer, and there's no key strokes, there's no mail, there's no postage. And this was, it's not new, it's been going on in the auto industry for quite a few years, but more and more retailers have wanted to get involved because the immediacy of getting the order in, and the response, and the whole issue of money, and turnaround. So we started four years ago, and I went to K-Mart in Michigan, and had a really nice training program, and we were going to bring them on first, and we came back and worked on the program, and all these things were very new to me. The idea of a network where you dial up, and you pick up your mail, and you'd have one customer, and you'd think of them as a file folder. And then, in the file folder, you'd have multiple envelopes. In one envelope would be an invoice, in one envelope would be an order, in one envelope would be a purchase order change, in one envelope would be an acknowledgment. And then, you'd have multiple customers, and you'd go out and pick up all your file folders, and then when you'd bring them in you'd split out the mail like a mailman. So it took a while to get that concept down and what it meant and how it was going to affect my company. And we brought it back, and we've worked on it, and we've implemented three customers so far.

Faculty: When you say "we," who do you mean?

Simpson: The outside software group, and myself, and of course, my operations staff now, because once it's implemented, then they dial up every day, and they do the day-to-day work on it. But "we" meaning me and the technical person from them. *But I set up the trading partnership with XYZ Electric, which is a, like I said, one of the three major networking groups. And I chose them because they were prevalent throughout all of our customers, so I wouldn't have to have multiple networks for different customers, I'd have one to represent us with all of this, so I set up a trading partnership, which is the legal document, and set up profiles, which is, just basically, how you're going to trade, and it's the technical stuff that they'll know that you're _____ and*

they're K-Mart or whoever.[Note 20] So we went, and we bought the commu-
nications portion and we set up the trading partnerships, and then we were
ready to test the software, and we would dial up, and pick up the test thing,
and bring it in, and right now, we have three customers who have multiple
documents, doing multiple versions of that document every year, they go up
a different version, like, 2001, 2002, 2003. And we've spent six figures doing
this, and this has been my project from scratch.[Note 21] And it's not done,
by any means, because we have twenty-two customers that want on this, and
it's a tremendous amount of effort, because of the fact that you're getting rid
of all the paper, so how do you know if it's correct? And so everything that you
do and plan for, obviously, the first one was the hardest, because you had to
think of every gotcha in the world from quantity and cost to description and
terms and all that. And I feel that that was a very effective project, and it still
is effective because I've gained knowledge, and it's making me more valuable
as an employee with them. And *it's adding to my market value as an individual*
in the marketplace because EDI is the thing, where now we're getting to the
point where, if we sell a toy to someone, when it comes into the toy store they'll
wand it, and that will tell them how many quantities they have, and then when
it goes out of their cash registers, they wand it, it deletes it from inventory
automatically, which creates an order, generates an order automatically,
which comes in electronically, and then, it's like a perpetual cycle.[Note 22]
And it's pretty slick. And technology-wise it's the in-thing and it's a very
volatile situation, and I like things ever-changing like that—always something
exciting.

Faculty: Okay. This sounds like the topic that we really want.

Take me through a part of it, a piece of it, where you thought you were
particularly effective.

Simpson: Okay. Customer calls and was turned over to me because they're
interested in EDI. They happen to be on the priority list. I talked to them and
explain to them where we're at, where . . .

Faculty: Can you give me one, one customer . . .

Simpson: Service merchandise.

Faculty: Okay.

Simpson: Okay? A woman named _____ called me up, and they happen to be
one of our five top customers, and it was agreed by the marketing group that
they were next in line. However, their stipulations are, you not only come up
on one document, you come up on all four documents, and you go paperless
within ninety days, which is very aggressive. *That is the most aggressive*
anyone's ever been. So I sat and explained to her where we were, where we'd
come in EDI and where we're at. And I was very effective in discussing it
because I had the knowledge behind it, and you wouldn't believe in this
business how many people don't know EDI. And this company happens to be
one of the older retailers that have been doing it for probably ten years, which
is all the older that it is in retail business. And I explained to her where we
were, and how we'd like to approach the situation, and could they try to bend

with us, and how we have our whole main-frame environment set up, and she said, that's fine. And I was effective because I had the knowledge in this case, and the fact that I had the right answers to her questions, and I was able to go and get the right answers if I didn't have them because of the fact that maybe it was a marketing issue. But we dealt with each other, and we worked it out, so I felt that in this specific instance, in dealing with EDI now, I'm effective because I have the knowledge, and I've already implemented one or two customers.[Note 23] Initially, when it was first done, I wasn't as effective as I am now. I was effective because I was the only person doing it, and people came to me, but in this case, it's really mutated to a different form of effectiveness now. And this install is going on right now. It's going on as we speak. It's in the test mode, which is, we're actually passing invoices and sending orders at the same time, and we should be going off of the test and into production in the next thirty days.

Faculty: Thank you.

[Self-Confidence]*[Note 24]*

Explanation of Coding Notes

Incident 1

Note 1: Persuasiveness, Indicator f. She is worried about her image. Because she has been working toward the promotion, she is expressing a concern for how the event would affect her recognition and promotion possibilities.

Note 2: Networking, Indicator a. She talks about a benefit of a training class being meeting other managers and operations people from various businesses all over the country. She mentions what she gets from these interactions, namely, a "flavor for the real world," and sees this as more valuable than the class itself. She is engaged in building relationships, which are work related. The relationships and interactions are helping her deal with work-related issues.

Note 3: Planning, Indicator c. She describes how she organized the binder/notebook by creating special tabs by category and what needed to be done. As she mentions, she may have to replace equipment or determine what was unusable, so placing the material in some order was important for her future application of the material from the class.

Note 4: Initiative, Indicator a. She scheduled visits to companies that had already made the transition to learn how they implemented the system. She says they were valuable to her. She learned from their mistakes. Because this was before "benchmarking" was a buzzword and a common practice in businesses, we infer that most people learning new systems and preparing to implement one in their organization might ask about other companies' experiences, but in 1989 or so, people may not have taken the time or trouble to go and visit the other companies.

Note 5: Repeat planning, Indicator b. She organized the cost information in a memo. It included the information and analysis needed by the financial people and was presented in a way to assist them in approving of it. She then moved it to the various people that had to approve and sign it. Although this would code under a different indicator than the previously observed incidents of planning, it would be considered a "repeat" and noted, but not counted in her *score* for planning. It was noted as a separate demonstration because it was not about the same aspect of the event. It was not about the binder.

Note 6: Repeat planning, Indicators a and e, and systems thinking, Indicator a. Planning: She set up the time schedule and a series of meetings to which she invited the various vendors and key internal people to evaluate software systems. The timetable established a specific goal or time deadline for the transfer to occur. Again, because this is a different aspect of the event, it is noted but not counted in her frequency score for this study. In other studies, the variations in demonstration of the ability in terms of the variety of behavioral indicators shown may be of interest, in which case these notations can be reclassified and analyzed for a different study at a later time. The description of the rationale for running parallel systems to avoid problems if the new system did not work properly would be coded for planning, Indicator e, under the concept of anticipating an obstacle and contingency planning. Systems thinking: She explains why she wanted to have the old and new systems running in parallel. In the description, she explains the possible causal sequence of problems that could occur.

Note 7: Efficiency orientation, Indicator b. She explains that when trying to justify something to someone, it is better to put it "in smaller pieces" than go for the whole thing at once. She says it is more effective for her as well. This comparative analysis and decision as to approach indicates a concern for doing it better than she had previously, or might have, and for maximizing her effectiveness in the presentation and project.

Note 8: Pattern recognition, Indicator d. She describes the interdependence in terms of a metaphor of a puzzle. She says it "kind of unfolds, and if you do it one piece at a time, you see it coming together."

Note 9: Attention to detail, Indicator a. She was concerned about being sure that she is doing everything she should be. She asked herself a series of questions to check herself. She was trying to reduce the uncertainty and *ensure* that the applications were running (i.e., operating) appropriately.

Note 10: Repeat planning, Indicator b. She describes the phases of the project in their sequence. She is describing the series of actions needed to get to the objective of the project.

Note 11: Repeat networking, Indicator a. This is not coded for her contacting previous clients of the vender. But her statement on forming ongoing relationships, what she calls "business partnerships," and the usefulness of these relationships indicates another incidence of networking.

Note 12: Empathy, Indicator a. She describes the man she was visiting in terms of his background, style, and behavior during her visit. She notes the consequences of his demeanor and the atmosphere he created. She explains that even when she was interrupted during their interview, it was not a problem because of the way he was dealing with her and the issues that came to him.

Note 13: Repeat systems thinking, Indicator a. She explains how she gathered all the information from the various vendors and sorted it into the parts she needed. Then she developed her cost justification memo according to their corporate practice, describing the rationale for the elements and method of presenting the information. She then describes the process for getting approvals. Again, as noted with planning and networking, this is a different aspect of the event than the previously coded systems thinking, so we would note it but classify it as a "repeat" demonstration because it is within the same incident.

Note 14: Duplication and elaboration of planning coded in Note 5. Although planning, Indicator e, is present in greater detail than it was in the segment discussed in Note 5, it is the same aspect of the event. She was worried about potential problems, so she was developing testing sessions and checklists and running the systems in parallel.

Incident 2

Note 15: Not coded for self-control. She lost control. Although she says she listened and did not say anything at first, she then says she "got piqued at him." She goes on in the following segment of the interview to describe how she was getting increasingly "curt" with him. Although she says it is not typical of her, she does say she was "pouncing on him" and "giving him heck." She also later got feedback from her boss after the person had lunch with her boss.

Note 16: Developing others, Indicator c, and empathy. Developing others: She asked the person why he didn't take the responsibility for an activity. When he responded, she explained about the prior training given to him and in other ways attempted to get him to change his behavior. The intent seemed to be to help the operations person change his behavior to one more appropriate to his job so that he would do his job better. If we thought the intent was merely to get the operations person to comply with her wishes, this might have been coded for persuasiveness. Empathy, Indicator b: She describes why the person did not take responsibility and intervene with the programmer-analyst. He felt that the programmer-analyst was handling the situation. She points out that the operations person is 15 years younger than the programmer-analyst and that his youth resulted in his not dealing with the situation directly.

Note 17: Pattern recognition, Indicator b. She relates the dynamics of this situation to a woman trying to "make my way in the business world" while male egos are involved. The current reluctance of the operations person and programmer-analyst to deal with her directly are positions she attributes to "male ego." She also goes on to describe how she is ineffective when these types of situations arise. The latter provides another theme or pattern that she identifies in this situation.

Note 18: Flexibility, Indicator a. As a result of reviewing the situation, she changed her approach and behavior significantly. She took the new approach and resolved the situation with the programmer-analyst. The longer segment is needed to fully observe the flexibility, but in the latter part of the segment we see another ability embedded—negotiating.

Note 19: Negotiating, Indicator a. She raised the issues during one of her regular lunches with the programmer-analyst. She explained her views and why she had approached the situation in that way. He offered his views and what he had said to her boss. They were then both able to "put their cards on the table" and resolve the situation.

Incident 3

Note 20: Efficiency orientation, Indicator d. She chose XYZ company because they were "prevalent throughout all of our customers" and she would not have to establish "multiple networks for different customers." This is a concern with best use of the resources.

Note 21: Systems thinking, Indicator a. She describes the causal sequence of events starting with the communications part of the agreement and partnership, which allowed the testing of the software. In the segment italicized with Note 21, she continues by explaining the benefits of this electronic data interchange (EDI) to their company and its interactions with customers.

Note 22: Continuation of the systems thinking first observed above.

Note 23: Persuasiveness, Indicators c and d. She was faced with a customer who took an aggressive position. She responded by explaining their capability, asking for a little "bend," and getting the "knowledge" the customer wanted to ensure the customer of the capability of the new system. She had the right answers to the customer's questions or was able to go and get the right answers. She wanted to convince the customer to use their new system.

Note 24: Self-confidence, Indicator a. Throughout all three incidents, Mary persevered and pushed ahead with her agenda. She entered into the various situations with an attitude that she was responsible and should take action. Although she was willing to apologize or reflect and acknowledge mistakes, she did not waiver in her actions or manner. This consistency provides the information with which to code her for self-confidence in this interview.

Summary of the Coding of Mary Simpson

For the research involved, there was the need to obtain a frequency score for Mary on each of the abilities as evident throughout the CII. Each ability was scored, if coded, up to a maximum of once per incident. The following abilities were coded for Mary Simpson in this interview:

⇨ Efficiency orientation—2
⇨ Planning—1
⇨ Initiative—1
⇨ Attention to detail—1
⇨ Flexibility—1
⇨ Empathy—2
⇨ Persuasiveness—1
⇨ Networking—1
⇨ Negotiating—1
⇨ Self-confidence—yes
⇨ Developing others—1
⇨ Systems thinking—2
⇨ Pattern recognition—2

Because this information is used in a development context as part of the course as well as the research, the feedback to Mary about the coding included three observations not evident in the frequency scores. First, she was observed—that is, coded—for many more of the people management abilities than is typical for entering MBA students. Second, she was coded as demonstrating the analytic reasoning abilities of systems thinking and pattern recognition more frequently than most entering MBA students *and* more than most effective middle-level managers.

Third, her demonstration of planning showed a great range in the sense that she was coded for four different indicators. Although the research was addressing only frequency of demonstration of the abilities, developmental coaching and building of her learning plan will be aided by the abilities, indicators, and ability-by-situation interactions shown. She should, for example, have a relatively easy time (as compared to her colleagues) constructing her learning plan and updating it as she proceeds through her MBA program.

CHAPTER SIX

Scoring, Scaling,
and Clustering Themes

Once you have developed a code or identified themes, you can use the information with a wide range of modes and methods of analysis. These can be seen as lying on a continuum from exclusively qualitative and verbally descriptive methods to primarily quantitative methods of statistical analysis. Points along the continuum may be quantitative description of the frequency of themes shown and other mixtures of methods.

To engage in quantitative description or statistical analysis requires a procedure for scoring the units of coding for each unit of analysis (for further distinctions among the units of coding and units of analysis, see Chapter 3). Whatever the procedure for moving the observations of themes into the analysis, the researcher may want to create groups of themes conceptually or quantitatively through clustering or scaling. Thematic analysis of qualitative information allows the researcher these options regardless of the method he or she has chosen.

Verbal Description

Using themes coded from raw information is conducive to verbal description of phenomenon, people, organizations, cultures, or events. Even if the researcher is conducting statistical analysis, aspects of the inquiry and its communication to others can be enriched through use of the qualitative "depth" of the thematic information available. The reader can become familiar with the people, organizations, or events under investigation by description of illustrative cases.

When the sample size is small or the study is of one organization (i.e., sample size of one), descriptive use of the thematic coding is desirable. Sometimes, at early stages of the inquiry, using thematic codes to describe the phenomenon helps the researcher focus, formulate hypotheses, or build a model of probable causality.

Descriptive use of the thematic analysis is also desirable if the methodology chosen for the study requires it (Wolcott, 1994). For example, not only do naturalistic inquiry, many applications of hermeneutics, deconstruction, and studies conducted from a postmodernist perspective recommend descriptive use of themes identified, but attempts to quantify the themes would violate conditions of the methodologies or values embedded in these methods. The proponents of such methodologies would contend that qualitative description is the only type of analysis appropriate. Typically, when there is no desire to generalize from the sample to others, or when the belief in the uniqueness of the people, organization, or event is strong, description of the units of analysis with the themes is desired and sufficient. Critics of such methods will often raise questions about whether the researcher's desire to "not generalize" is sufficient. They might claim that the researcher should guard against the prospective reader's tendency to violate this condition and to generalize observations, findings, or conclusions— but that is another argument and not within the bounds of this book to pursue.

Descriptive or interpretative methodologies do not preclude scoring or scaling of themes and then using this numeric representation to check the consistency of judgments (i.e., reliability; see Chapter 7). Neither do they preclude using the information to portray the themes and describe the units of analysis (Wolcott, 1994). Researchers early in their career or eager to prove their inclusion in a professional reference group may take a narrow interpretation of such methodologies as rejecting all use of numbers, even for descriptive purposes (such as the use of percentages). But security in one's self-esteem and experience as a researcher often results in less rigid positions.

Quantitative Translation

If one has a sufficient sample size and has addressed relevant sampling issues (see Chapter 3), thematic analysis allows one to translate one's qualitative codes into numeric representation. This can then be used for quantitative description of the units of analysis and/or analysis through the use of statistical routines. The quantitative translation can also be used for hypothesis testing. This application typically follows the code development studies as a later stage in the inquiry about the phenomenon.

Scoring Themes

Once themes have been identified, if there is the desire to describe or analyze the observation with numeric representation, a procedure for scoring must be adopted. Scoring of thematic codes takes one of five forms: (a) nominal; (b) presence or absence; (c) frequency conditioned on the coding of presence or absence; (d) frequency without the above condition; or (e) intensity.

Nominal or Presence/Absence Scoring

Nominal scoring is determining which of two or more coding options is satisfied. For example, a code for gender that includes two categories, male and female, calls for a nominal scoring of the qualitative information. The unit of analysis (i.e. the person) is scored as either male or female. One is not necessarily greater or better than the other unless you are pursuing a political or genderist theory.

For another example, imagine a code of marriage rituals as based or not based on Christian beliefs. In this case, the researcher might be looking for the mention of Jesus Christ as the Savior or Son of God, or the Blessed Mary as the Mother of God as parts of the theme. A particular ritual observed could be nominally scored as Christian or not Christian on the basis of the mention of or allusion to Jesus or his Mother.

When the theme is truly nominal, scoring and coding become the same act. To observe the theme in the raw information is to score it. But sometimes it is uncertain whether the categories are really ordinal or whether they are viewed as ordinal by the researcher. Although the researcher may claim that the coding categories or scoring options do not represent a hierarchy (i.e., one category is not better or higher or greater than the other category) an ordering or ranking of the coding or scoring may appear *because there is a ranking or ordering inherent in the groups of the units of analysis.* In other words, an ordinal property may be imbedded in the criterion variables or dependent variables used to group the raw information and units of analysis.

For example, suppose you have developed a thematic code from applications to psychology Ph.D. programs differentiating those who had graduated versus those who had not (or more accurately, not graduated, let us say, within 12 years of admission). Suppose one of the themes was " Mentions a specific psychological phenomenon of interest for future study with evidence of having pursued background reading in the literature," you would read the application essays and code an applicant as having "demonstrated this theme" or "not." While this might seem like nominal scoring, it is really ordinal. You were using a code developed to predict which Ph.D. applicants were likely to complete their dissertations and graduate, versus become ABD (All But the Dissertation). As a faculty member in an academic department about to devote a great deal of time and energy to the development of each student in the doctoral program, you want to select applicants who have a likehood of graduating. Aside from the political or philosophical discussion as to whether this approach to screening applicants is too utilitarian, and the contention that completion of a graduate program is each student's own responsibility, most faculty with doctoral programs engage in some form of this discussion about their screening and admission process. Although we may contend that an individual who completes a Ph.D. program is not necessarily a "better person" than someone who does not, and there may be "real world" factors that may cause someone to become ABD, the criterion used to develop the code has a hierarchy. The faculty engaged in this pursuit, consider a person showing this theme in their application essays to be a "better" candidate. In this way, a theme that appears to call for a nominal scoring, in actuality, calls for an ordinal decision in the scoring.

When the categories are ordinal, or in some cases when they are nominal, the scoring is determining the presence or absence of the theme. In this situation, the absence of an observed theme *implies* that something is missing. Often the presence of the theme is assumed to be either distinctly more desirable or distinctly less desirable (i.e., to be a sign of something good or something bad). For example, in scoring certain coding systems that describe a developmental scheme or hierarchy, a theme indicating each stage may call for presence-or-absence coding, but the final score for the person may be the highest stage coded as present. In such a scoring scheme, a score of Stage 4 would imply that a person was missing evidence of Stage 5.

Frequency Scoring

The third type of scoring is the use of a "presence" code for one theme that leads to the coding for other "subthemes." For example, when coding need for achievement, need for affiliation, or need for power (Atkinson, 1958; McClelland, 1985; Smith et al., 1992; Winter, 1973), the researcher examines a Thematic Apperception Test (TAT) story for the respective motive imagery. In other words, if the researcher observes and codes the first TAT story of a subject as having need-for-achievement imagery, then he or she goes on to examine that story in relation to the 10 subcategories of the need-for-achieve-ment motive code. The imagery is coded as present or absent, but the subcategories are not coded unless the imagery is first coded as present. The method of scaling (to be discussed later in this chapter) involves the number of subcategories coded as present to be added to the subject's score of 1 on need for achievement.

In such situations, the initial presence-or-absence coding is more power-ful in determining the eventual total score for the unit of analysis than each of the subthemes. Although the final score may look like an interval scale (and elements of it are, such as the subcategory score), overall, it does not show a vital property of an interval scale. That is, a score of 4 is not the same conceptual distance from a score of 3 as the score of 1 is from the score of 0. Therefore, the resulting numeric score should be treated like an ordinal score rather than an interval one.

Some frequency scores derived from thematic codes also have properties like those of an ordinal scale rather than an interval scale. For example, the coding for empathy used as the example in Chapter 5 is a frequency code. The subject is coded for demonstrating empathy once per incident of the interview. The number of times it is coded for a person becomes his or her score of empathy. The person may show empathy from zero to six times if six critical incidents are solicited during the interview. But the typical distribution of empathy in a sample is not random; it is often referred to as a "sideways J-curve" distribution (i.e., it looks like a "J" tilted 90 degrees). In other words, many of the units of analysis will show a score of 0, a lesser number of units of analysis will show a score of 1, substantially fewer units of analysis will show a score of 2, and scores of 3 or more will be relatively rare. In such a case, the scored thematic code should be treated as an ordinal number for purposes of analysis.

In many quantitative methodologies, algebraic and arithmetic transfor-mations are used to reconstitute the distributions as normal before statistical analysis. In many qualitative studies, the desire of the researcher for descriptive use of the data as well as inferential testing suggests that transformation, such as logarithmic or square root transformation, will result in scores that do not make visual sense. Nonetheless, such transformations can be used to normalize the scores if sample size is sufficient and other sampling issues have been addressed.

The fourth type of scoring is the use of a frequency score that is truly an interval scale. This often requires not only the likelihood of a normal distribution but also the likelihood that the total number of units of coding examined for each unit of analysis will provide sufficient instances of the phenomenon to be coded. This increases the probability that the scores will result in a normal distribution. (See Chapter 3 for a detailed discussion of units of coding and units of analysis.)

For example, in coding of historical documents, such as political speeches, a sentence may be used as a unit of coding (Winter & Healy, 1981), and the researcher may decide that a theme cannot be coded in two contiguous sentences. (Such a rule of coding, often called a coding protocol or procedure, may be established conceptually or empirically. Once it is established, it should be used in future research with that specific code until additional research shows it to be unnecessary or changes it.) In this example, a 20-minute speech (if you can find a political speech that short!) might have 40 pages of transcript and an average of 13 sentences per page for a total of 520 sentences. It might be possible to code a particular theme over 200 times! This coding choice alone may result in a different distribution than if you chose to code the particular theme only at the opening and closing of a speech. The latter decision would allow the theme to be coded twice at most as compared to 200 times. Choosing and developing coding protocols, units of coding, and scoring techniques will affect the possible distributions of the resulting scores and thus the types of analysis that can be conducted with them.

Intensity Scoring

The fifth type of scoring is an intensity score. An intensity score will seem like the fourth type, a frequency score that is truly an interval score. The distinction may be more conceptual or theoretical than empirical.

For example, a researcher may be coding an audiotape of a department's weekly staff meeting. Suppose that one of the themes is a code for "positive affect about the organization" or "pride in the organization" and that the unit of coding is each 5-minute period of the 1-hour staff meeting. The resulting score of each staff meeting could be considered an intensity score. That is, the score would represent the intensity of the "pride" or "positive affect" of the staff regarding the organization or department.

Intensity scoring may be a part of the code. That is, the code may specify levels of the theme. If these levels reflect an internal scale and not a developmental scale (like coding with a stage model), the coder assigns an intensity score at the time of examining the unit of coding.

Intensity scoring of themes may require adjustments for characteristics of the raw information that provide or allow additional opportunities to show the codable theme. For example, suppose your raw material comes from autobiographical essays written without an administered time limit. If you are examining each sentence for the presence of one of the themes in your code, a person who wrote a longer essay will have more opportunities to be coded for each theme. If you are using the number of times that a theme with positive affect appears as an indicator of the person's intensity of positive affect (i.e., if you are using a frequency code as an indicator of intensity), then the length of the essay is a potential source of bias in the raw information. You may want to examine length of the essay as another variable, but to study properly the intensity of positive affect, you should adjust the intensity score of the theme by the length of the essay. A simple method might be to divide each person's score by the number of pages. But this assumes that everyone was typing the answers. If some were handwritten and some typed, then adjusting by the number of sentences would be a more accurate adjustment for opportunity.

Simple Scaling

The researcher may find him- or herself with a variety of themes that appear to have a relationship with each other. A conceptual or empirical relationship may be predicted by the underlying theory or may become apparent during the code development process. The vehicle for reflecting or examining these relationships could be scaling or clustering. Although these two words can be used for similar operations, *scaling* will mean the combination of two or more coded themes into a single score, whereas *clustering* will mean the organization of multiple themes into groups. A scale is the "theme" on which raw information is being coded, whereas a cluster is a higher-order theme, or metatheme. Clustering is a form of organizing your data to help in analysis or interpretation (Coffey & Atkinson, 1996). Miles and Huberman (1984) claimed that "clumping together things" into clusters is a process of moving to higher levels of abstraction and facilitates presenting of qualitative information. Whether a simple scale or a cluster is formed, the aggregation of themes may be an interim step during the process of analysis as well as during interpretation.

A scale can be created from the simple addition of several themes. Another variation is a presence/absence decision followed by a straight sum of other subthemes, as in the procedure described above for the scoring of motives called *need for achievement, need for affiliation,* and *need for power.*

A simple scale can also be constructed from alternate indicators, as in Chapters 2 and 4. The example in Chapter 5 used a code in which two or more "alternative manifestations" of a competency were listed for each competency. These were called the *behavioral indicators* of the competency. Each one described a behavior or action that might be observed in the sample being coded (in Chapter 5, it was an incident in a critical incident interview). The underlying theory of competencies (Boyatzis, 1982) postulated that each competency might be demonstrated in various situations by slightly different but related behaviors. For the purposes of scoring, therefore, each behavior would be considered an alternative indicator of the competency. If a subject demonstrated two different indicators of the competency of empathy in the same incident, he or she would still be scored only once for demonstrating empathy.

Another method of scaling behavioral alternatives is found in the "just noticeable differences" scaling of Spencer and Spencer (1993). First developed for use in a job-skill forecasting project (Boyatzis & Schaalman, 1985), it arranges the various behaviors associated with a competency in a sequence suggesting a developmental hierarchy. In Spencer and Spencer's (1993) study, the hierarchy was considered one of complexity or sophistication in demonstration of the competency.

For example, in the code shown in Chapter 5, for a competency called *group management,* three of the five alternative behavioral indicators are:

(a) creates symbols of group identity, pride, trust, or team effort; (b) acts to promote commitment to a team, task, or shared goal through friendly, personal contact; and (d) allows the group to take responsibility for certain task accomplishments and does not assume personal responsibility for them.

In Spencer and Spencer (1993, pp. 61-62), Indicator (a) above would be seen as indicative of Level 6 within the competency of teamwork and cooperation;

Indicator (b) would be indicative of Level 3; and Indicator (d) would be indicative of Level 5. Spencer and Spencer would say that Indicator (a) of creating symbols of group identity or pride was a higher-order aspect of a person using this competency that required greater facility or a more advanced capability with this competency.

Although there are many types of scaling, a traditional quantitative version of scaling involves the computation of factors or clusters of variables and then using this empirical structure to calculate scores. This will be discussed in the next section as a part of clustering.

Forming Clusters of Themes

Forming clusters of themes may be useful as a way to organize the code: that is, to organize the array of themes identified (Coffey & Atkinson, 1996). It may also be useful in the transformation of the data to aid in the analysis, whether descriptive or empirical.

Clusters of themes may be important for the presentation of the findings or in the formulation of further research or application. The method of forming clusters, or organizing themes into larger categories, asks the researcher to choose from primarily two different approaches: (a) organizing the themes on the basis of a theory or conceptual framework or empirically and (b) organizing the themes in the context of other themes, as independent clusters of themes, or in a hierarchy.

Conceptually Organized Clusters

As the researcher discovers themes in the qualitative information, his or her ability to conduct thematic analysis and recognize patterns does not stop. There is a natural continuation of the quest to search for patterns in the themes. Many of the same personality, learning style, cognitive orientation, and other factors discussed earlier in Chapter 2 are associated with a researcher's disposition toward a favored approach to development of a code. The same characteristics leading him or her to theoretically driven or prior-research-driven or data-driven code development will affect a researcher's degree of satisfaction with a list of themes. They will also push him or her to find the most "elegant" organization of the themes.

If the thematic analysis is a part of an early stage of inquiry into the phenomenon, then the researcher's own bias will probably determine the type of organization sought. If the thematic analysis is part of a later stage, earlier research will have an impact on whether conceptual or empirical clusters are used.

Conceptual or theoretical formation of the clusters might use (a) related characteristics, (b) identification of an underlying construct, or (c) a causal or developmental hierarchy. As an example, we will examine the competency research before and after development of the thematic code presented in Chapter 5.

The earlier research on which this code was primarily based appeared in Boyatzis (1982). In this study of more than 1,000 practicing managers, one sample was studied to determine their views about competencies related to superior performance as a manager. Another sample was studied to identify competencies demonstrated through various tests and behaviorally demonstrated in the critical incident interview (called the "behavioral event interview") as related to measures of the same managers' performance. Colleagues and myself at McBer and Company worked on the separate job competency studies that later formed the database for the study published in 1982 in *The Competent Manager: A Model for Effective Performance* (Boyatzis, 1982).

Before publication, the first five complete drafts of the manuscript of *The Competent Manager* presented the data on each of the competencies organized on the basis of a conceptual framework of "related characteristics." All of the competencies related to interpersonal interactions were placed in a cluster called the "interpersonal cluster," those related to analytic or cognitive processes were placed in the "intellectual cluster," and so forth. The left-hand column in Table 6.1 shows the competencies reported in the book in their four original, conceptually organized clusters: the entrepreneurial cluster, the interpersonal cluster, the intellectual cluster, and the socioemotional maturity cluster.

Two other methods for conceptually organizing the themes, which in this case were competencies, into clusters could have been used. Themes can be conceptually organized through the identification and application of an underlying construct. For example, for many years, occupational classification systems followed the Department of Transportation (DOT) system, which uses "data," "people," and "things" as three underlying variables with which to classify the skill needs of every occupation.

TABLE 6.1   Comparison of Theoretical Versus Empirical Clusters From
                Boyatzis (1982)

Theoretical Clustering	Empirical Clustering
Entrepreneurial:	*Goal and Action Management:*
Efficiency Orientation	Efficiency Orientation
Initiative	Initiative (i.e., Proactivity)
Interpersonal:	Diagnostic Use of Concepts
Concern With Impact	Concern With Impact
Use of Unilateral Power	*Directing Subordinates:*
Developing Others	Developing Others
Managing Group Process	Use of Unilateral Power
Use of Socialized Power	Spontaneity
Oral Presentations	*Human Resource Management:*
Intellectual:	Managing Group Process
Diagnostic Use of Concepts	Use of Socialized Power
Logical Thought	Accurate Self-Assessment
Conceptualization	Logical Thought
Socioemotional Maturity:	*Focus on Others:*
Stamina/Adaptability	Perceptual Objectivity
Accurate Self-Assessment	Self-Control
Perceptual Objectivity	*Leadership:*
Spontaneity	Oral Presentations
Self-Control	Self-Confidence
	Conceptualization

Another example using the types of competencies discussed in Chapter 5 could involve organizing the competencies into clusters that were "driven by" similar unconscious motives or traits. For example, if the need-for-achievement motive (McClelland, 1961, 1985) was used as an underlying construct, we might say that efficiency orientation, planning, and initiative could be clustered together. Each manifests a behavioral component related to the need-for-achievement motive, in which a person has an unconscious desire to "do better" and "strive for improved performance or conditions against some standard of excellence." Efficiency orientation, as defined and described in the codebook in Chapter 5, is the expressed concern about doing better. Planning, as described in the same codebook, is organizing things or actions to get something done. Initiative is starting something or doing something in a unique way. All three competencies involve trying to do something and could be interpreted as based on an underlying need for achievement. Spencer (1995) described a "periodic table" of competencies expanding on the theory proposed earlier in Boyatzis (1982) that identified the motive or trait levels of competencies. Once the deeper, unconscious levels are identified, the behavioral or skill levels are listed as clusters around these underlying constructs. This approach has also been referred to as the "atoms and molecules concept" of competence. The separate competencies are like atoms, which are clustered into forms, like molecules, in which they appear in work or social settings.

A third approach to conceptual clustering is to organize the themes into a hierarchy. The researcher is asking, Do some of the themes lead to or cause other themes? Is there a developmental hierarchy embedded in the list of themes? If this is true, some of the themes would appear to feed or enable other themes, such as would appear statistically in path analysis.

Continuing with the example used in this section, the competencies involved with analytic or cognitive processes could be organized into a cluster based on cognitive complexity. In such an organization, memory would be the simplest level (Boyatzis, 1982). Use of concepts, or basic deductive reasoning, would be the next step. Systems thinking, which reflects thinking in terms of multiple causal relationships, would be the next level. Perceiving and thinking in terms of multiple causal relationships require many basic deductive relationships. It requires use of concepts as applied to many different sets of associations.

Moving to higher levels of cognitive complexity, we could place pattern recognition, or the inductive process of identifying themes or patterns in seemingly unrelated information, as the next highest cognitive capability. It would be impossible to perceive patterns inherent in complex data or seemingly unrelated data without the ability to build, perceive, and think in terms of multiple causal relationships (i.e., systems thinking, or the previous lower level). Pattern invention, which could be called theory building, could be placed at the highest level of such a hierarchy. Recognizing patterns within data would be a cognitive building block for a person's ability to imagine the array of data and invent or create a new pattern of theory.

Spencer and Spencer (1993) organized behavioral indicators of each competency into a "just noticeable difference scale," as described earlier. This method of organization was a developmental hierarchy, originally produced conceptually.

Conceptually organizing clusters of themes is the easiest method for the researcher, although not necessarily the most useful nor empirically valid. It is easy for the researcher because it arrays the themes in terms of the researcher's theory. What is in his or her mind drives the clustering. Of course, the clusters make sense to the researcher! Using this approach to creating clusters also enables linkage to other theories and possibly prior research *because it is organized in the way that researchers think about their phenomenon.*

This approach has some limitations. First and foremost, it may not reflect the interrelationships among the themes. It also does not necessarily reflect the way the phenomenon described by the themes occurs in life. For example, the related characteristics approach, the underlying construct approach, or the developmental hierarchy approach to organizing the competencies into clusters does not necessarily reflect the way a human engages and uses his or her talent and capabilities. This leads us to the major alternative method for creating clusters of themes—empirically.

Empirically Creating Clusters

There are a variety of statistical vehicles, from descriptive to multivariate, for creating clusters of themes. Descriptive methods involve using histograms, scatter plots, or graphs to array the themes along one or more numeric distributions. If the sample size is sufficient, the scoring of the themes appropriate, and the distribution of scores appropriate to the conditions, various multivariate statistical routines can aid in this approach.

Returning to the main example used in this section about competencies, a multivariate analysis of the data revealed a different grouping of the competencies than the conceptual approaches to creating clusters did. Cluster analysis was chosen as most appropriate to the data in the Boyatzis (1982) study. It showed five clusters: the goal and action management cluster, the directing subordinates cluster, the human resource management cluster, the leadership cluster, and the focus-on-others cluster. The competencies are shown in these empirically derived clusters in the right-hand column of Table 6.1.

Mentkowski, McEachern, O'Brien, and Fowler (1982) studied a female sample of middle-level managers with the same critical incident interview and thematic codebook that Boyatzis (1982) developed on a predominantly male sample. With one exception, they found the same competencies significantly related to superior performance as a manager. But they found that among the exclusively female sample, the empirical clusters were different. In the Mentkowski et al. (1982) study, accurate self-assessment was associated with the goal and action management cluster instead of concern with impact; stamina and adaptability were associated with concern with impact and use of socialized power; and positive regard was associated with developing others and managing group process. According to the authors, the dynamics resulting in the different empirical clusters reflected important and evident differences in the situations faced by female managers in the late 1970s and early 1980s in the United States. These distinctions would have been lost to the researchers if they had used a conceptual method for creating the clusters.

The empirically developed clusters allowed the theory presented in Chapter 2 of *The Competent Manager* (Boyatzis, 1982) to be expanded and elaborated in later chapters. In Chapter 12 of the book, the clusters of competencies could be linked to job functions and element of the organizational environment. These connections were essential to further research of the theory and design of applications.

For example, all of the competencies involving "people interaction" were conceptually placed in the interpersonal cluster. It was difficult to link this cluster to the functions of management, such as planning, organizing, controlling, motivating, and coordinating. At the same time, the empirically derived cluster called the *directing subordinates cluster* contained the competencies of developing others and use of unilateral power. This cluster of competencies could be related to the controlling and motivating functions of management and to specific components of the organizational environment. Presentations of the competency model with the empirically derived clusters appeared to make sense to executives and human resource professionals. These individuals were sensitized to seeing a manager's capability in the context of his or her job and the organizational environment. Presentations of the competency model to research psychologists appeared to make sense with either the conceptual or the empirical organization of the competencies.

Empirical approaches to creating clusters help by revealing the interrelationships of the themes as they appear in the data or the scoring of the themes. They may also reveal underlying constructs not originally evident to the researchers. The major limitation of such approaches is that often researchers are using thematic analysis at early stages of inquiry into a phenomenon. This often results in working with small samples and scores whose distributions violate basic requirements for the appropriate use of multivariate statistical routines.

For example, if you use a criterion variable to identify and select your sample, factor analysis may reveal a clustering of themes embedded in your criterion variable. You are getting an "empirical reflection." This mirroring effect does not reveal a clustering of your theme; it merely reestablishes the criterion variable with which you selected your sample. This is particularly evident in extreme-case designs, in which criterion variables are used to select samples, such as looking for superior-performing managers and average-performing managers.

Further, multiple regression or discriminant function analysis will be inappropriate if you do not believe or predict your themes to be mutually exclusive. If you expect the themes to have some conceptually meaningful interrelationships, then multiple regression will distort these relationships by forcing them out of each successive step in the regression. The resulting clusters will have an inherent property that you, in this example, will see as inappropriate.

In relation to the major example used in this chapter, the study of a person's competencies related to managerial effectiveness begins with the theory that human beings have a set of interrelated capabilities. We might contend that initiative and persuasiveness would be related. When a person uses his or her initiative to instigate a new project, he or she will be attempting to influence others to accept the project, see it as valuable, and possibly join the project team. Forcing these two competencies to be mutually exclusive, independent, or orthogonal is an artificial imposition on the way the researcher would expect the themes to appear in practicing managers.

Similarly, discriminant function analysis assumes that the second discriminant function is independent of the first. The researcher may predict or want to allow for the possibility that the clusters of themes are systematically related in a conceptually meaningful manner. Using statistical routines that force independence of the clusters will distort the analysis and misrepresent the clusters of the themes.

A Brief Review

The researcher may want to use the themes and code to describe the units of analysis or phenomenon without further processing the themes. In such situations, the themes and code become the descriptive material, with illustrative examples from the raw information. If the researcher wants to use quantitative techniques to describe, analyze, or interpret the phenomenon, there are a variety of methods for scoring, scaling, and clustering the themes that have been discussed in this chapter and are summarized in Table 6.2.

TABLE 6.2   Summary of Techniques for Empirically Scoring, Scaling, and Clustering Themes Within a Code

---

Types of Scoring

1. Nominal (generating nominal data)
2. Presence or absence (generating ordinal or possibly nominal data, depending upon the concepts in the theme)
3. Frequency based on a preliminary presence-or-absence scoring (generating ordinal data)
4. Frequency (generating ordinal or interval data, depending on the technique of counting the frequency and concepts in the theme)
5. Intensity (generating interval data)

Types of Scaling

1. Adding themes, or subthemes within a theme
2. Listing alternate manifestations as items to be counted or scored, not merely as indicators of a theme
3. Statistically computing scales based on statistical procedures, such as factor scores

Methods of Clustering

1. Theoretically defining the clusters, which may be done on the basis of:

   a) Related characteristics

   b) An underlying construct

   c) A hierarchy

2. Empirically determining the clusters
3. Defining the themes in the context of other themes
4. A hierarchy

CHAPTER SEVEN

Reliability Is
Consistency of Judgment

$\mathbf{R}$eliability is critical in using thematic analysis. Reliability is consistency of observation, labeling, or interpretation. It is *not* verification, which is a pure, positivistic notion. It affects the potential utility of the code and the research findings that result from the use of the code. It affects the potential for replication, extension, and generalizability of the research. Validity of findings cannot conceptually exceed the reliability of the judgments made in coding or processing the raw information.

Reliability as Seen From
Various Epistemological Perspectives

Various perspectives are used to label differences in how researchers view the world and determine the nature of good work. While these are differences in epistemology, "paradigms" is a concept often used to explain or describe these differences. The literature provides arguments for quantitative versus qualitative, positivistic versus organic, and universalistic versus postmodern paradigms, to name a few.

Sometimes one is struck with the genuine differences—much more than divergence—in the ways people construct the world and determine what is true or valid. Other times, such distinctions are used in territorial disputes among researchers and academics who have no other way to say elegantly, "I don't like how you think!" or "I disagree with you!" In such situations, relatively small differences between two researchers can be blown up to gargantuan proportions in the effort to establish differences. Meanwhile, from the outside, the differences are so small as to seem negligible. Advancement of science, knowledge, and research does not seem to be served by such exaggeration. On the other hand, once eloquently made, the arguments may make sense.

This chapter discusses reliability as an issue of importance to most, if not all, paradigms for understanding and using qualitative information (Mason, 1996). It will attempt to bridge some of the rifts opened up by debates over small differences and differences that are merely semantic.

Converting themes into codes and then counting presence, frequency, or intensity does not in and of itself create a link between qualitative and quantitative methods (Creswell, 1994). The computation or articulation of interrater reliability, or convergence of perception of multiple judges, must occur as well. As described by Creswell (1994) and discovered by most of us, the linkage is desirable because it allows researchers to combine the richness and uniqueness of qualitative information with the precision and discipline of quantitative methods.

When people from different countries who speak different languages meet for the first time, a translator facilitates communication. Thematic analysis is a translator. With reliability as consistency of judgment, thematic analysis provides for methodological translation and conceptual bridges between two or more approaches to discovery.

Positivist social science and interpretive social science can be viewed as two substantially different paradigms (Silverman, 1993). Thematic analysis allows the interpretive social scientist's social construction of meaning to be articulated or packaged in such a way (with reliability as consistency of judgment), that description of social "facts" or observations seem to emerge. The identification of these observations satisfies the positivist social scientist's conceptual definition of discovery. The reverse process can assist the interpretive social scientist in understanding the special and distinctive qualities of observations made by the positivist social scientist through thematic analysis.

Thematic analysis with reliability allows the interpretive social scientist to generate qualitative hypotheses that provide a basis for a positivist social scientist to conduct qualitative or quantitative hypothesis testing as part of the building process of science. Whether you call this combining of methods a conceptual bridge or a Satanic perversion, it begs for new labels. Miller and Crabtree (1992) went so far as to call it qualitative positivism. Thematic analysis also allows the opposite process. The hypothesis testing of a positivist social scientist can be viewed as generating observations or themes that the interpretive social scientist can then use for exploration.

According to Kirk and Miller (1986), reliability from a traditional, positivist perspective—what they called "quixotic reliability"—"refers to circumstances in which a single method of observation continually yields unvarying measurement" (p. 41). Although such test-retest reliability may inspire confidence in the dependability of the measurement method, it is associated with relatively insensitive measures, as will be discussed at length later in this chapter. Kirk and Miller also described two other types of reliability: diachronic and synchronic. Either or both may be more appropriate to a particular inquiry or stage in the research process than quixotic reliability.

Regardless of ontology or epistemology, a code, a codebook, and an assessment of consistency of observation provide

1. Reliability for the positivist or postpositivist
2. Dependability for the postmodernist
3. Ability to communicate with others (i.e., engage in social construction) for the hermeneutic, interactionist, or relativist
4. Ability to interact with others about observations (i.e., dialogue or conversation) to the relationist

Without the above possibilities, interpretation is only a discussion pleasing to theorists that leaves out the richness of the qualitative information. If the reader feels the need to explore in greater depth the differences between various epistemologies, Denzin and Lincoln (1994) have provided a thorough explanation of the philosophical roots of various approaches. Often the qualitative researcher is forced away from issues such as the importance of consistency of judgment because of the heavy-handed way in which positivists of the past have used their arguments to deny a voice to qualitative richness. Just think about methodological rigor and "correctness" of the consequences of this type of heavy-handedness as aversive conditioning in other aspects of life!

Consistency of Judgment

Reliability is consistency of judgment that protects against or lessens the contamination of projection. Consistency of judgment with qualitative information appears in two basic forms: (a) consistency of judgment among various viewers; and (b) consistency of judgment over time, events, and settings.

Consistency among Viewers

Consistency among various viewers is attained when different people observing or reading the information see the same themes in the same information. *Interrater reliability* is consistency of judgment among multiple observers. Kirk and Miller (1986) called both of these forms of consistency of observation *synchronic reliability,* given that it refers to similarity of observations made within the same time period by multiple observers. *Rater-to-expert reliability,* also termed *category agreement with an expert* (Holsti, 1968; Smith, 1992), is consistent with specific other individuals who have authored previous research, discovered themes, and developed a thematic code.

Consistency of judgment among viewers is dependent on the access of the multiple coders to the raw information. Thus, the reliability, not to mention the validity, of information obtained in qualitative research is directly affected by the *way* the information is recorded and the choice as to *what* is recorded. Audiotape and videotape recording help reduce variation in observations by creating a consistent source of the qualitative information. The researcher can view or listen to the tapes many times. He or she can ask colleagues to view or listen to the tapes many times. The group of researchers can review the tapes together and discuss the coding of moments during the tapes.

Other aspects of research design and methods affect consistency of judgment of the information for code development or coding. For example, standardization of the interview protocol or stimulus can increase the consistency of judgment of the raw information by increasing the consistency of the setting in which the qualitative information is collected. Achieving comparability of samples, settings, and other issues of sampling units of analysis involves more than just searching for comparison groups. It involves ascertaining information from the various people, organizations, moments, or whatever forms the units of coding and the units of analysis in a way as to increase the feasibility of determining consistency of judgment among multiple observers or researchers.

Consistency Over Time and Events

Consistency over time and events is attained when a person makes the same observation at two different times or in two different settings. Although

Kirk and Miller (1986) called this *diachronic reliability,* the usual label is *test-retest reliability.* Given that the intention of qualitative research is often to "discover" something about the phenomenon or its uniqueness or to investigate the rich variety of experience inherent in a setting, the question of stability of the phenomenon over time seems almost inappropriate to ask.

For example, test-retest reliability, the most commonly used, asks if the measurement method shows the same result when assessing something over two different assessment sessions or time periods. Thus, asking someone if she is alive or dead will typically produce the same answer at the beginning and the end of a 2-week period. But this perspective on reliability pushes the researcher toward measurement methods with high stability but low sensitivity. For example, suppose that this person just had a grueling 2 weeks working toward deadlines for a company going through a downsizing. Meanwhile, she has been preoccupied by a family crisis because her father is dying of cancer. She may be feeling considerably different after these 2 weeks. Although she may still answer that she is "alive," the question hardly touches on the degrees of feeling "dead" or "alive." Granted that the question being asked is not "What is your relative mood state?" But many researchers are so preoccupied with attaining the Holy Grail of test-retest reliability that they sacrifice the sensitivity of their measures.

Such inappropriate use of reliability results in a widespread rejection of reliability as a relevant issue in most qualitative research. Hopefully, the ideas raised in this chapter will help to restore the discussion to the appropriate issues of consistency of judgment and ways to think about improving it or increasing confidence in consistency of observation.

Though test-retest reliability seems inappropriate for most qualitative research, it does bring up the important issue of comparability of samples (Smith, 1992). In most qualitative research, a "retest" or repeat of the phenomenon of interest does not occur naturally. Therefore, when test-retest is imposed on a design, it creates an artificial assessment with its own arousal effects. In this sense, administering the assessment instrument or method twice to the same people at different times or in different settings may in and of itself create an arousal and an additional field experiment.

Researchers using the Thematic Apperception Test (TAT) have observed a sawtooth effect in a person's responses to the same stimulus at various times. The TAT is a projective test in which a person is asked to tell an imaginative story in response to looking at a picture. The sawtooth effect is the observation that a person will remember his or her specific imaginative stories and consciously override the instruction, which is to tell the first story that comes to mind, seeking instead to tell a different story (Smith, 1992). The resulting low test-retest reliability has frequently been cited as a reason for disregarding research using the TAT and claiming its instability as a measurement method. Winter and Stewart (1977) tested the accuracy of this conclusion directly by administering TATs with the typical instructions and two conditions with modified instructions. In the modified set, the person was either instructed to "try to put yourself in the state of mind that you were in when you wrote stories to these pictures. Try to rewrite stories as much as possible like the ones you wrote before" or to "not worry about whether your stories are similar to or different from the stories you wrote before." In either of these modified cases, Winter and Stewart (1977) found that the test-retest reliability increased significantly to levels well within accepted standards.

The experience of taking a projective test is like many experiences studied in qualitative research. The measurement moment is a rich, human experience engaging many aspects of the person. This "engagement" may result in recollection of the moment of measurement, which then creates an additional arousal stimulus at the next attempt to assess the person. Multiple episodes of producing thought, behavior, or interacting with others are not independent samples of information from a person or setting. Thus, the repeat administration of a measurement method does not constitute an assessment of test-retest reliability because the situation measured becomes a new situation.

Although we may disregard test-retest reliability as inappropriate for much qualitative research, comparability of sample selection within a study remains an important methodological issue. To discover, investigate, or assess a person, organization, or culture, it is desirable to be exposed to and to examine as much variation as possible. In other words, if we wanted to assess a person's skills through observation of the person at work, we would want to observe him or her in various types of situations at work over a number of different days, weeks, or months. A person's demonstrated skills may be different while talking to an angry colleague or subordinate than when talking to a customer. His or her demonstrated skills may be different on the day he or she returned from a 4-week vacation than on the last Friday of the month. As discussed in Chapter 3, sampling for comprehensiveness is crucial. It allows for maximum variability within the raw information and the most complete picture of the unit of analysis. The essential point is that design of sampling in qualitative research should be driven by concerns for comprehensiveness rather than test-retest reliability.

Confidence in Judgments as a Form of Reliability

Although statistics uses "confidence" as part of another concept (i.e., confidence intervals), the word can also be applied to a researcher's belief or trust that he or she has captured the phenomenon under investigation and that his or her judgments are sound. In this sense, increased confidence in one's observations can be considered a form of reliability. Zyzanski, McWhinney, Blake, Crabtree, and Miller (1992) asserted that reliability is equivalent to credibility and dependability, as compared to validity, which is closer to confirmability. Silverman (1993), in expanding this notion, pointed to Jick's (1979) concept of triangulation as a way to achieve reliability. When we find similar observations by multiple observers, we feel more "confident" that the observation is a sound one rather than a momentary delusion or personal, subjective perception. To the positivist, it still remains to be determined that the shared similar view is something more than a socially constructed perception resulting from the convergence of thought and values emanating from a "tight" or strong culture. That is, does this similarity of observation result from relatively independent judgments, or is it "group think" at work? To interpretivists, such convergence is always a function of shared social construction. They would not need further evidence of dependability. A number of these authors of texts and articles on qualitative methods agree that reliability is aided by multiple observations, multiple observers, and using multiple samples to be observed (Jick, 1979; Mason, 1996; Silverman, 1993; Zyzanski et al., 1992). No one claims that such techniques entirely remove reflexivity and make the multiple judgments independent audits. The quest is typically for *increased confidence* in the dependability of the judgments without the preoccupation with or the illusion of "objective" judgments.

Methods of Attaining Reliability

Double Coding

Perhaps the most used technique for attaining reliability or, more correctly, sufficient reliability to proceed with the analysis and interpretation is double coding (Miles & Huberman, 1984). In this technique, two people observe the raw information or events at the same time if they occur in real time or independently if they are recorded in written, audio, or videotaped form. Each person makes judgments without interacting or seeing the judgments of the other observer. Following the observation period or completion of the judgments, the two observers compare their results. In the simplest form of double coding, the two observers discuss each observation until agreement is reached. The same process can be followed with three, four, or more observers.

The discussion leading to the agreement of the various observers will be affected by the influence skills, mutual trust, interpersonal styles, and cognitive styles of the observers. If one of the observers is more forceful in his or her assertions, his or her observations may be taken as the consensus, not because they reflect everyone's best judgment but because the individual is more persuasive. This dynamic is also plagued by other possible sources of confusion or contamination. For example, differences in communication style by gender (Case, 1988) or perceptions of differential skill or expertise may result in the pair, trio, or group's allowing one observer to dominate the decision-making process.

The observing process is also an arousal process. For example, in the research described in Chapter 2 about the effects of alcohol consumption on aggressive behavior of men, the coders of the videotapes found themselves arguing, not only about differences in their judgments, but about when to take lunch breaks, how to arrange the room being used for watching the videotapes, and other issues. The hours spent watching men drinking and acting aggressively had aroused a degree of aggression in the observers. A third researcher often had to act as a third-party negotiator to resolve differences in judgment about the coding.

Given the variety of concerns about double or group coding mentioned, it seems useful to ascertain the degree of similarity and consistency of judgment of the independent observers and coders before their efforts to reach consensus. This helps the researcher determine the degree of difficulty in applying the code and may suggest revisions in the code or recycling of the code development process before continuing onto the analysis phase of the research. It also helps the reader of the research to assess the degree of interpersonal influence needed to achieve agreement on the final observations used in the analysis.

Independence of Judgments

The various ways to assess the degree of initial agreement, or lack thereof, of the observers or coders are often referred to as ways of assessing interrater reliability. In situations in which the coders are relatively equal in their experience of using the code and/or experience with the raw information or situation being observed, finding a way to measure their degree of agreement before reconciliation discussions is useful.

In some research, one person may have previously developed a code and used it in numerous studies, and now another coder is trying to learn the original researcher's code and coding protocol. In others words, there is a great difference between the expertise of the two coders with the code. If one or more new researchers are trying to learn a code as it was developed and has been used in previous studies, then the agreement of the new coders with the original research is referred to as rater-expert reliability. It follows the same process as interrater reliability, but a set of "correct" (in reality, relatively "more correct") answers to the judgment situations have already been ascertained. The new coders are then judged against this expert standard.

Measures of Interrater or Rater-Expert Reliability

There are two basic forms of interrater and rater-expert reliability: percentage agreement and correlation. Of the possible variations in the calculation of percentage agreement scores, two appear most popular in the literature: (a) percentage of agreement of all judgments as a function of opportunity and (b) percentage of agreement as to the presence of the coded theme. Of the possible variations and correction equations in calculating correlations, three appear most popular in the literature: (a) the Pearson product moment, (b) Kendall's tau, and (c) Spearman's rho. Each of these has different conditions under which it is appropriate to the phenomenon being studied and the type of code being used.

To assist in exploring these differences, three pairs of coders' judgments will be used in illustration. The example is taken from typical distributions of coding critical incident interviews from executive MBA students (like those in Chapter 5). In this example, three pairs of different coders' judgments of 30 managers' demonstrated empathy as coded from critical incident interviews are shown. The codebook reported in Chapter 5 was used to code empathy. These initial judgments from each pair are shown in Table 7.1. It is important to note that the data were based on typical distributions. The pattern of coding of each pair was developed to illustrate issues involved in calculating reliability, not to provide information comparing six independent coders. Statistical summary of the distribution of each coder's scores is shown in Table 7.2. Coder C and Coder D differed from Coder A and Coder B in that

TABLE 7.1   Six Coders' Frequency of Observation of Empathy From 30
Subjects' Critical Incident Interviews

Subject	Coder A	Coder B	Coder C	Coder D	Coder E	Coder F
1	0	0	0	0	0	0
2	1	0	1	0	0	0
3	2	1	2	0	1	0
4	1	1	0	1	1	0
5	2	2	3	3	2	2
6	0	0	0	0	0	0
7	0	0	0	0	0	0
8	0	0	0	0	1	0
9	1	1	0	1	1	0
10	0	0	0	0	0	0
11	1	1	1	0	1	0
12	2	2	2	2	2	1
13	0	0	0	0	0	0
14	0	0	0	0	0	0
15	1	1	1	0	1	0
16	0	0	0	0	0	0
17	1	2	0	2	1	1
18	0	0	0	0	0	0
19	1	1	3	3	1	1
20	0	1	0	1	0	0
21	0	0	0	0	0	0
22	0	0	0	0	0	0
23	0	0	0	0	0	0
24	2	2	4	4	2	2
25	2	2	1	2	1	2
26	1	0	0	0	1	0
27	2	2	3	1	1	1
28	0	0	0	0	0	0
29	0	0	0	0	0	0
30	1	2	0	1	1	0

they saw empathy in fewer of the managers but saw it more frequently within
a manager when it was found. Coder E and Coder F had a substantial
difference in the number of managers for whom they saw or coded empathy.

Percentage Agreement

Percentage agreement is often used by qualitative researchers when the
number of themes coded are few, the number of observed situations (i.e., units

TABLE 7.2   Descriptive Statistics About Each Coder's Views of the Sample of 30
                Subjects

Variable	Coder A	Coder B	Coder C	Coder D	Coder E	Coder F
Mean	.700	.700	.700	.700	.600	.333
SD	.794	.837	1.179	1.119	.675	.661
Kurtosis	−1.120	−1.269	1.343	1.745	−.517	2.048
Skew	.610	.636	1.581	1.596	.693	1.820
Range (min-max)	0-2	0-2	0-4	0-4	0-2	0-2

of coding) are few, or the researcher is "antistatistical" and does not want to involve him- or herself with a computer. Aside from the last reason, which is clearly an attitude or a consequence of an epistemological socialization problem in the narrowness of the position taken, the former two reasons suggest that percentage agreement is more appropriate than correlations. Also, if the data resulting from coding will most likely be nominal or ordinal, percentage agreement scores will be more appropriate than correlations (Cohen, 1960).

There is another and most important reason to use percentage agreement scores as estimates of reliability: The themes being coded call for "yes/no" or "presence/absence" judgments by the coder. Because many of the interpretive, thematic codes require a presence/absence judgment by the coder, percentage agreement is the most typically cited measure of interrater or rater-expert reliability.

Percentage agreement scores can be calculated as the number of times of observation or coding in which the two coders agree divided by the number of possible observations, or instances of coding. The equation is:

$$\text{Percentage agreement} = \frac{\text{no. of times both coders agreed}}{\text{no. of times coding was possible}}$$

This seems most appropriate when the unit of coding and unit of analysis are the same. This is a percentage agreement score regardless of whether the raw information is coded as "present" or "absent."

A popular variation on percentage agreement scores is percentage agreement on presence (Atkinson, 1958; McClelland, 1961, 1985; Smith, 1992). In this variation of the above formula, there is the assumption that coding a theme as present is more important than coding a theme as absent. This may occur because the phenomenon of interest only makes theoretical sense when it occurs. The absence of the coded theme does not imply the opposite of presence, or there is not an equal likelihood of observing presence and absence. The equation is:

$$\text{Percentage agreement on presence} =$$

$$\frac{2 \times (\text{no. of times both Coder A and Coder B saw it present})}{(\text{no. of times Coder A saw it present} + \text{no. of times Coder B saw it present})}$$

For example, in the illustration being used here, a person may be coded for having demonstrated or shown empathy in an incident in the interview. If a person is not coded for having shown empathy in an incident, we do not know if this implies that the person does not typically demonstrate empathy. In other words, it may be a competency that he or she does not use or was not using here. The incident being reported may not involve another person, so that it would have been difficult to demonstrate empathy. Or the person may have focused on the noninterpersonal aspects of the incident. In this case, the absence of empathy may be a meaningful observation about the relative lower value that the person, in this context, placed on using empathy as compared to other abilities.

A contrasting example might be coding for gender. If the research is using a code based on a theory of two genders, male and female, then coding for the presence of one is the same as coding for the absence of the other. In this case, the earlier percentage agreement score would be sufficient to capture the reliability or consistency of observation of the coders.

Frequency of occurrence or observation also affects the appropriateness of the measure of reliability chosen. Few occurrences of the codable phenomenon increase instability and decrease meaningfulness of reliability for some codes. Bales (1970) discussed the instability caused by analyzing the position of a person in the coalitions within a small group with his interaction process analysis and SMYLOG because of infrequent codable interactions involving that person. The same issue applies to the measurement of reliability. Smith et al. (1992) claimed that all forms of reliability other than straight percentage agreement are misleading when occurrence is infrequent. It can also be noted that in terms of the arithmetic, infrequent coding will result in a relatively low denominator in the "percentage agreement on presence" formula. A small change in agreement or lack of agreement will change the percentage dramatically—thus leading to the instability of this measure of consistency of judgment.

In the example shown in Table 7.1, Coder C and Coder D were different than Coder A and Coder B in that they observed empathy less often in the managers. The mean for all four coders was the same. Coder C and Coder D saw empathy in 10 and 11 of the 30 managers in the sample, respectively. Meanwhile, Coder A and Coder B saw empathy in 15 and 14 of the managers, respectively. But as evident in the averages shown in Table 7.2, Coder C and Coder D saw empathy more frequently when they found it at all; their range was 0 to 4. The range for Coder A and Coder B was 0 to 2.

Table 7.3 shows the coders' various percentage agreement scores. Straight percentage agreement suggests that Coders A and B are reasonably consistent. Typically, scores of 70% or better are considered necessary in this type of research. When percentage agreement treating presence and absence as equivalent is examined, all three pairs of coders appear acceptable.

Prior research (Boyatzis, 1982; Boyatzis, Cowen, & Kolb, 1995; Boyatzis et al., 1996) with the code used in this example has shown that this form of empathy is infrequently observed in managers (i.e., less than half of the time) when the critical incident interview is used or when managers are observed in real-time interactions. Therefore, percentage agreement of "presence only" seems more appropriate. When this measure of reliability is used, the pair of Coder A and Coder B showed considerable consistency at 90%, but the pair of Coder C and Coder D did not at 57%; nor did Coders E and F at 64%. A researcher would feel more confident in the coding of Coders A and B than in the coding of Coders C and D or Coders E and F. If both sets of coders were able to reach 100% agreement after discussion of coding disagreements, there would have been less likelihood that interpersonal influence and stylistic differences between the coders within each pair were affecting the consensus scores of Coders A and B than that they were affecting Coders C and D or Coders E and F.

Coders E and F had similar ranges, 0 to 2 for each manager with whom they found empathy, but they differed substantially in how many managers they coded for empathy. Coder E saw it demonstrated by 15 of the managers, a number similar to that reported by Coders A and B, but Coder F saw it in only 7 of the managers. The percentage agreement on presence only for Coders E and F falls below acceptable levels at 64%, reflecting their lack of consistency. If we allowed the absence of empathy to be considered as the conceptual equivalent to presence, we would find acceptable levels of reliability of Coders C and D, as well as Coders E and F. But this seems misleading, for they apparently are relatively less consistent than Coders A and B. In this

TABLE 7.3   Comparison of Various Forms of Calculating Interrater Reliability

Measure	Coders A & B	Coders C & D	Coders E & F
% Agreement[a]	80%	63%	67%
% Agreement of presence and absence[b]	90%	70%	73%
% Agreement of presence only[c]	90%	57%	64%
Pearson product-moment correlation	.846	.740	.696
Kendall's tau correlation	.804	.483	.631
Spearman correlation	.848	.528	.659

NOTE: For all correlations and measures of association, $N = 30$.
a. % Agreement = no. of times agreed / 30
b. % Agreement = no. of times agreed it was present or absent / 30
c. % Agreement of presence = 2 × (no. of times both agreed on presence) / (no. of times A saw it present + no. times B saw it present)

example, overall, both of these pairs do not seem as adequate in terms of consistency as Coders A and B.

Correlations

Three correlation coefficients are used with coded data to determine interrater or rater-expert reliability: Pearson product moment, Kendall's tau, and Spearman's rho. The Pearson, which is the most commonly used correlation coefficient in general, assumes interval data with a normal distribution. The Kendall's tau is a measure, often called a rank-order correlation, "based on counting the number of times that pairs of things are in the same versus opposite order on both variables" (Cliff, 1996, p. 29). The Spearman's rho "converts the scores into ranks and computes a Pearson correlation between the ranks" (Cliff, 1996, p. 29). Li, Rosenthal, and Rubin (1996) reported formulas to increase the accuracy of reliability estimates using these types of correlations. They explained that these measures of reliability often contain errors because of inappropriate assumptions taken as applicable by researchers.

First, the researcher should assess the nature of his or her data on the basis of the type of thematic code being used, the sampling, and the resulting scores. Although some scores may appear to be interval scores, the coding protocol may mean that scores are more ordinal than interval in nature. For example, TAT scores of the motives of need for achievement, affiliation, or power are really ordinal scores. The coding of each is based on a presence or absence judgment as to "imagery" preceding the search for subcategories. Once subcategories are found, a person's motive score for a picture (i.e., the unit of coding) is the sum of the imagery and number of subcategories found. The motive scores are closer to ordinal than interval scores (McClelland, 1985; Smith et al., 1992). In other words, a coder determines the presence or absence of motive imagery, and then and only then does he or she proceed to code for subcategories. Although a person's score on one of the motives could range from 0 to 11 on the need-for-power motive, the difference between a score of 1 and a score of 0 is different than the difference between a score of 8 and a score of 7 on the coding of the motive in a picture of the TAT. These motive scores do not reflect normal distributions with any populations studied.

Recall the example used in Chapter 5 of coding for abilities from critical incident interviews. A person is coded once per incident for each of the abilities. The person's score on a particular ability from each of the incidents in the interview is added to the others: That is, incidents are summed to give a score on his or her ability. So a person's score on empathy can range from 0 to 4 from an interview in which four incidents are solicited. Examination of the distribution in Table 7.2 shows a non-normal distribution from any of the individual coders, as is evident in the raw scores shown in Table 7.1. The distribution of scores is closer to a geometric than a normal distribution. Therefore, it would be safer to assume that the scores have properties of ordinal data rather than interval data. Nonparametric correlations are often chosen for such data.

In our current example, the Pearson product moment, Kendall's tau, and Spearman's rho correlation coefficients are shown in Table 7.3. The Pearson appears to be high for all three pairs and, in the case of Coders C and D, appears higher than any other measure of reliability. Meanwhile, the Kendall's tau is the lowest for each pair, suggesting it either has the most distortion or is the most conservative of the correlations and other measures of association. Due to the number of 0 scores from all of the coders, any of the correlation coefficients seem less appropriate than percentage agreement scores. If we were to ignore this issue and choose one of them, the Kendall's tau would seem most appropriate because of the inherent ordinal nature of the data (Cliff, 1996).

TABLE 7.4 Summary of Recommended Options for Determining Consistency of Agreement or Reliability

Coding Decision for Scoring Each Unit of Analysis	Resulting Type of Data or Scores	Measure of Consistency of Agreement or Interrater Reliability
Yes or no; presence or absence	Nominal	% agreement
Yes or no; presence or absence; frequency; ranking	Ordinal with normal or linear distribution	% agreement
Yes or no; presence or absence; frequency; ranking	Ordinal with geometric distribution or infrequent occurance	% agreement of presence
Frequency; intensity; rating	Interval with an embedded go/no decision or a non-normal distribution	Kendall's tau or Spearman's rho
Frequency; intensity; rating	Interval with normal distribution	Pearson's product moment

Summarizing the Options for Calculating Reliability

All options or issues involving consistency of judgment and determination of reliability have not been addressed in this chapter. Each researcher must come to a decision based on his or her data, sampling, code, unit of coding, unit of analysis, and nature of the coding decisions. Given the most common thematic codes and coding process, the recommended options are summarized in Table 7.4.

CHAPTER EIGHT

Don't Go Breaking My Heart

Challenges in Using Thematic Analysis

There are two major categories of challenges facing those who wish to use thematic analysis—personal challenges and those for the field, discipline, or profession. To curious researchers frustrated by the lack of "insights of consequence" produced through single-method designs or those of us facing maddeningly elusive phenomena, these challenges represent major obstacles to progress in our inquiry (and potentially forces inhibiting our publication productivity!).

Before beginning the discussion of challenges, a brief review of definitions may be useful. The definitions of thematic analysis, a theme, a code, and a codebook are shown in Table 8.1. Thematic analysis is a process that can be used with any form of qualitative research.

Descriptive use of thematic analysis is desirable if the methodology chosen for the study requires it (Wolcott, 1994). Descriptive or interpretative methodologies do not preclude scoring or scaling of themes and then using this numeric representation to check the consistency of judgments. Neither do they preclude using the information to portray the themes and describe the units of analysis (Wolcott, 1994). Often, using both aspects of thematic analysis enhances the clarity of results or findings and ease of communication.

In addition, thematic analysis allows a researcher with a qualitative method and design to develop themes and a code, use a check on consistency

TABLE 8.1 Definitions

Thematic analysis is a process for encoding qualitative information. The encoding requires an explicit "code."

A *theme* is a pattern found in the information that at the minimum describes and organizes the possible observations or at the maximum interprets aspects of the phenomenon. A theme may be identified at the manifest level (directly observable in the information) or at the latent level (categorizing issues underlying the phenomenon).

A *code* may be a list of themes; a complex model with themes, indicators, and qualifications that are causally related; or something in between these two forms.

A *codebook* is the compilation or integration of a number of codes in a study.

Three methods of developing themes are
1. Initially generating themes inductively from the raw information
2. Initially generating themes deductively from theory
3. Initially generating themes from prior research

of judgment (i.e., reliability), do scoring and scaling, and then apply statistical analysis to the determination of validity of the themes or code. In the latter case, the researcher has not violated any tenets of qualitative methods but has provided a way to communicate with researchers who prefer quantitative methods. In providing access to discoveries and insights generated through qualitative methods, use of thematic analysis extends and expands the possible audience for the communication and dissemination of ideas and results. Thematic analysis also allows a researcher using quantitative methods to incorporate operant and open-ended measures or forms of information collection into their designs.

Regardless of all this potential, thematic analysis is not easy to use. Like any qualitative method, if conducted properly, it typically takes more time and energy than quantitative techniques.

Personal Challenges

To the experienced scholar using qualitative methods and thematic analysis, the challenge is easy to describe. It is the Michael Jordan imperative, "Just do it!" But to the scholar early in his or her career, questions arise about using thematic analysis with various qualitative methods: How long does it take? What problems do you find? What can go wrong? What do I do when I feel stuck? For the scholar who is experienced in using qualitative methods but has not engaged all of the aspects of thematic analysis described in this book, the questions are more focused: What can I gain in using additional aspects of thematic analysis? How will it help in my discovery process? What additional aspects of the phenomenon will more complete use of thematic analysis generate? These are questions about utility and incremental insight.

There are two other types of scholars with possible interest in qualitative methods and using thematic analysis—the midcareer scholar and the researcher whose career has focused on the exclusive use of quantitative methods and inferential analysis. A midcareer scholar is somebody who has been studying a phenomenon for a number of years and is feeling somewhat bored or restless with it. What do you do? Other than buying a red sports car, entering a Zen monastery, or experimenting with other solaces to midlife and midcareer crises, the opportunity might be to dramatically change the methodology with which you have been approaching your phenomenon! For you, this introduction to thematic analysis may enable you to explore various qualitative or quantitative, functional or organic, experimental or inductive research designs.

To the scholar who has never used qualitative methods, and therefore not used thematic analysis: Think of walking along city streets late at night with your coat pulled tight to keep out the cold or damp air or to lessen that sense of vulnerability. Someone emerges from an alley and whispers, "Psst, psst, hey, you wanna try something exciting?" Although the typical response is to avoid such encounters, if there is some part of you that flirts with the idea, "Wouldn't it be fun, just once, to say yes and see what happened?" then you may want to try different methodologies—dramatically different methodologies—and discover new dimensions to your phenomenon or new paths in your inquiry!

Now think back to the old British television series *Monty Python's Flying Circus*. They would open each show with the intriguing invitation: "And now, for something completely different. . . ." Even if you are not in that restless state of wanting to break out and try new methods, you may be curious about the facets of your phenomenon as yet undetected by the methods you are currently using. The teacher played by Robin Williams in the film *Dead Poets Society* instructed his students to explore poetry by standing on top of their desks in class! This was not the usual approach to the subject, especially for an all-male private school in the 1960s. It led to different perspectives on things they saw every day, and that sometimes led to different insights about the world around them.

I Can't Get No Satisfaction

Like all research, sometimes thematic analysis does not result in any discoveries, findings, or results! Of course, after spending all those hours immersed in the raw information, the researcher does emerge with a greater in-depth "sense" of the raw information. The difficulty is determining the source or meaning of the lack of findings. Some of the most likely problems were addressed in Chapters 3 and 7. Problems in the sampling of criterion or dependent variables, sampling of raw information, and sampling of units of analysis and units of coding can all be contributing to a paucity of findings. In addition, there is also the possibility of mistakes in the form of data collection.

Toward the end of my graduate school years, I decided to conduct a laboratory experiment to develop a code for two types of power motives. At the time, those of us studying such things were calling them "socialized" and "personalized" power. The arousal and comparison conditions were carefully designed and pilot tested for "manipulation checks." The subject solicitation and incentives were tested for appropriateness of subject candidates responding and willing to participate. The sample size was carefully constructed, as was the experimental setting and random assignment to conditions.

The thought patterns to be used to develop a thematic code differentiating the two types of unconscious/conscious power imagery were from a Thematic Apperception Test (TAT). To update the pictures and stimulus value of the pictures in the TAT (after all, it was 1970, and the existing pictures used in research were from the 1950s or earlier!), new pictures were selected. Because the design called for comparable samples of men and women subjects, pictures were selected that involved men and women, as well as people of different racial and ethnic groups. The data collection went smoothly during the summer of 1970 in Cambridge, Massachusetts.

Months later, when repeated attempts to discover a thematic code differentiating the arousal conditions failed, I showed the raw information to colleagues. They could not find anything. Then I showed it to my thesis advisor (this was not a part of my thesis but a separate study), David McClelland. After about an hour of reading and discussing some of the stories written in response to the TAT pictures, David stopped and looked at me from across the table. Lowering his reading glasses, he said in that low voice ominous to those of us seeking support or professional verification, "What pictures did you use?"

The summer of 1970 was a tumultuous time in Harvard Square and Cambridge, as it was throughout the United States. People were protesting regularly, burning draft cards, bras, and police cars. There was an atmosphere of chaos amid claims of repression and oppression. The specific pictures used in this version of the TAT had evoked images of the struggle going on around us. This arousal of the time and place was much stronger than the experimental arousal conditions. The failure to generate a thematic code and produce interesting discoveries and findings was rooted in a data collection problem.

Research is a process of discovery and, at times, searching for validation or refutation of observations. If it always produces predicted findings, either it is not research or it is examining a trivial phenomenon. Of course, there is always the possibility that the researcher is so brilliant that his or her work always produces valuable insight!

Using thematic analysis does not ensure meaningful results or observations. With all of the cautions and issues described in this book, I consider finding some meaningful themes in three out of every five studies to be a reasonable expectation, even when using the techniques that meet the conditions described in preceding chapters. Often in one out of those three studies in which some meaningful themes were identified, I feel that the number of themes or the depth of interpretation possible with the themes identified is not satisfying. As with most research, when findings do not emerge as you expect, you can still learn about the phenomenon, data collection methods (as in the example above), sampling, and other aspects of the research design or the "thing" being studied.

I Could Have Danced All Night

In Chapter 3, the discussion of sampling addressed issues of efficiency as to the amount of time involved. It takes longer to do qualitative research than most other forms of research. Using thematic analysis may lengthen or shorten the time a researcher spends with the raw information. Searching for meaningful observations and attempting to extract all of the important discoveries can lead a researcher to months of exploration of the raw information. Careful design and consideration to sampling units of analysis and coding can provide the researcher with the opportunity to use thematic analysis and decrease the amount of time involved in data processing. With most forms of recorded raw information (i.e., written, audiotaped, or videotaped), code development could take 2 to 3 days. The more complicated the phenomenon and the more channels of information available in the raw data, the longer this will take.

For example, developing a code from videotapes of groups takes longer than developing a code from paintings or prayers used to open convocation ceremonies. The videotapes have the content of what is being said by each person; the reactions of others to it; each person's emotions, body posture, gestures, and other nonverbal reactions; pair and coalition interactions within the group; fantasies or values shared by the group and representing the entire group; and so on and so on.

The same issues apply to application of a thematic code. Of course, in studies using a previously developed or an existing code, the researcher typically has the benefit of prior experience with the phenomenon, sample, and data collection methods. Such prior experience enables the researcher to carefully design the minimum number of units of analysis and units of coding needed to discover, establish, or prove the questions and/or hypotheses driving the inquiry.

If You Can't Be With the One You Love, Love the One You're With

If you are not a scholar with experience in various qualitative methods, you are probably asking, "Why bother? This seems like a lot of work with a possibility of little to show for it." Unfortunately, this type of logic has dominated the hidden dialogue about research in the social sciences, and particularly the behavioral sciences, for 50 years. It seems easy to design a questionnaire asking a respondent to rate or rank a number of items. Administer it to a large number of people. Enter the data and run the programs. The longest part of producing a publishable paper using this approach is the review of the literature—or possibly waiting for the reviewers' comments after submission to a journal! These perceptions of time efficiency raise a question as to whether the goal of the research is insight and understanding or publications per month.

The personal challenge is also a challenge to all of our fields, disciplines, and professions about research. We should use ingenuity and creatively study the phenomenon of interest directly.

I Can See Clearly Now

Early in the use of qualitative methods and systematic thematic analysis, researchers are often drawn to the manifest level of analysis. This is an important level of analysis, but it is not the only level! Current books and articles about computer programs that aid qualitative analysis (Weitzman & Miles, 1995) provide useful tools for data linking, using hypertext to develop and apply codes to written source material, or branching through CD-ROM to video and audio source material. Here, again, there is a tendency to draw the researcher to the manifest level. While this is the level of interest for various linguistic and ethnographic analyses, for most qualitative methods, the latent *and* manifest levels hold the gems of insight. An interpretive analysis of latent themes allows for the fullest sense of the context as a referent or basis for understanding the phenomenon. Although recent computer programs can assess semantic context and even interpret syntax, they still lack some of the contextual understanding that a person is capable of using.

Not long ago, an article in the *Wall Street Journal* ("Stamping out TV Violence," 1993) raised issues and joined in the controversy about how to curtail media violence. From *The Power Rangers* (Boyatzis, Matillo, & Nesbitt, 1995) to action adventure series, movies, and even *Beavis and Butthead,* the dilemma is whether exposure to violence on television arouses or legitimizes violence by children, teenagers, or adults. Studying the arousal versus cathartic effects of television and movie violence has led to interesting observations: For example, exposure to violence in the daily news has more of an arousal effect on behavior for children than fantasized violence, and people denied a typical dosage of television, including the violence, demonstrate increased antisocial behavior and psychosomatic symptoms of illness (Baker & Ball, 1969; Feshbach & Singer, 1971). Meanwhile, certain social advocacy groups have attempted to impose restrictions and labeling of shows to allow parental control, or the illusion of control, over children's viewing behavior.

Despite the considerable research literature about film and television from a qualitative and interpretive perspective (Rowland & Watkins, 1984), the primary measurement method used has been counting the number of violent acts per show, per hour, per minute, per protagonist, and so forth. This is thematic analysis at the manifest level. The contention of the *Wall Street Journal* article is that 40 years of counting violent acts has not helped to reduce violence in our society, on movie screens, or on television. The meaning, context, causes, and consequences of violence are all important considerations in understanding the phenomenon. What is needed is more frequent and visible thematic analysis at the latent level as well as the manifest level. But like research designs using only questionnaires asking respondents to rate the phenomenon of interest, counting violent acts is easy, and there are minimal questions raised about interrater reliability or consistency of judgment.

Challenges to Our Field, Discipline, and Profession

Whether these comments are seen as challenges or merely requests for consideration, a growing number of researchers are asking for, requesting, and sometimes expecting mixed-method inquiry in the social sciences. Thematic analysis allows some of this and provides a language and techniques for scholars to venture into methodologically new arenas. Because most of the underlying issues have been discussed at length in earlier sections of this book, I will not explain the rationale for each one. As a reader of research on many diverse topics with many diverse methods, and as a professor watching and trying to help emerging scholars early in their careers develop habits of curiosity and research to help create insight, I have come up with the following challenges to the social sciences.

1. Can we help scholars to "see?" That is, can we help researchers break out of the frameworks and assumptions about legitimate sources of information and open their eyes to the richness of information around them every day?

2. Can we help transform the qualitative-versus-quantitative debate into a challenge to our creativity and ingenuity as observers and researchers?

3. Can we help researchers, observers, and practitioners develop skills in code development and to appreciate the importance of reliability in using and applying thematic codes?

4. Can we help create an environment for collaborative research in which thematic analysis can be conducted appropriately? Like most qualitative research, thematic analysis takes too much energy, time, and concentration for one person to do alone. In addition, we need the perspective of multiple observers to test the clarity of our articulation of the themes that we believe we see, to interpret the meaning of these themes, and to communicate and help others learn how to use qualitative methods to gain insight.

References

Abell, W. (1957). *The collective dream in art: A psycho-historical theory of culture based on relations between the arts, psychology, and the social sciences.* New York: Schocken.

Atkinson, J. W. (Ed.). (1958). *Motives in fantasy, action, and society: A method of assessment and study.* New York: D. Van Nostrand.

Baker, R. K., & Ball, S. J. (1969). *Mass media and violence: A report to the National Commission on the Causes and Prevention of Violence.* Washington, DC: Government Printing Office.

Bales, R. F. (1970). *Personality and interpersonal behavior.* New York: Holt, Rinehart & Winston.

Boyatzis, C. J., Matillo, G., & Nesbitt, K. (1995). Effects of *The Mighty Morphin Power Rangers* on children's aggression with peers. *Child Study Journal, 25,* 192-227.

Boyatzis, R. E. (1973). *Alcohol and aggression: A study of the interaction.* Unpublished final report on Contract No. HSM-42-72-178, submitted to the National Institute of Alcohol Abuse and Alcoholism. Rockville, MD.

Boyatzis, R. E. (1974). The effect of alcohol consumption on the aggressive behavior of men. *Quarterly Journal of Studies on Alcohol, 35,* 959-972.

Boyatzis, R. E. (1975). The predisposition toward alcohol-related interpersonal aggression in men. *Journal of Studies on Alcohol, 36,* 1196-1207.

Boyatzis, R. E. (1976). Power motivation training: A new treatment modality. *Annals of the New York Academy of Sciences, 273,* 525-532.

Boyatzis, R. E. (1982). *The competent manager: A model for effective performance.* New York: John Wiley.

Boyatzis, R. E. (1983). Who should drink what, when, and where if looking for a fight. In E. Gottheil, K. A. Druley, T. E. Skoloda, & H. M. Waxman (Eds.), *Alcohol, drug abuse and aggression* (pp. 314-329). Springfield, IL: Charles C Thomas.

Boyatzis, R. E. (1995a). Cornerstones of change: Building the path for self-directed learning. In R. E. Boyatzis, S. S. Cowen, & D. A. Kolb (Eds.), *Innovation in professional education: Steps on a journey from teaching to learning.* San Francisco: Jossey-Bass.

Boyatzis, R. E. (1995b). Stimulating self-directed learning through the Managerial Assessment and Development Course. *Journal of Management Education, 18,* 304-323.

Boyatzis, R. E., Baker, A., Leonard, D., Rhee, K., & Thompson, L. (1995). Will it make a difference?: Assessing a value-added, outcome-oriented, competency-based professional program. In R. E. Boyatzis, S. S. Cowen, & D. A. Kolb (Eds.), *Innovation in professional education: Steps on a journey from teaching to learning.* San Francisco: Jossey-Bass.

Boyatzis, R. E., Cowen, S. S., & Kolb, D. A. (Eds.). (1995). *Innovation in professional education: Steps on a journey from teaching to learning.* San Francisco: Jossey-Bass.

Boyatzis, R. E., Leonard, D., Rhee, K., & Wheeler, J. V. (1996). Competencies can be developed, but not in the way we thought. *Capability, 2*(2), 25-41.

Boyatzis, R. E., & Schaalman, M. (1985). *A developmental model of competency needs of the workforce: Report to the governor of the state of Connecticut as part of the Jobs for the Future Project.* Boston: McBer.

Bray, D. W., Campbell, R. J., & Grant, D. L. (1974). *Formative years in business: A long term AT&T study of managerial lives.* New York: John Wiley.

Campbell, D. T. (1988). *Methodology and epistemology for social science: Selected papers.* Chicago: University of Chicago Press.

Campbell, D. T., & Fiske, D. W. (1959). Convergent and discriminant validation by the multitrait-multimethod matrix. *Psychological Bulletin, 56,* 81-105.

Campbell, D. T., & Stanley, J. C. (1963). *Experimental and quasi-experimental designs for research.* Chicago: Rand McNally.

Campbell, J. (1949). *Hero with a thousand faces.* New York: World.

Campbell, J. P., Dunnette, M. D., Lawler, E. E., III, & Weick, K. E., Jr. (1970). *Managerial behavior, performance, and effectiveness.* New York: McGraw-Hill.

Case, S. S. (1988). Cultural differences not deficiencies: An analysis of managerial women's language. In S. Rose & L. Larwood (Eds.), *Women's careers: Pathways and pitfalls* (pp. 41-63). New York: Praeger.

Cliff, N. (1996). *Ordinal methods for behavioral data analysis.* Mahwah, NJ: Lawrence Erlbaum.

Coffey, A., & Atkinson, P. (1996). *Making sense of qualitative data.* Thousand Oaks, CA: Sage.

Cohen, J. (1960). Coefficient of agreement of nominal scales. *Educational and Psychological Measurement, 20,* 37-46.

Colby, A., Kohlberg, L., Speicher, B., Hewer, A., Candee, D., Gibbs, J., & Power, C. (1987). *The measurement of moral judgment: Vol. 2. Standard issue scoring manual.* New York: Cambridge University Press.

Crabtree, B. F., & Miller, W. L. (Eds.). (1992). *Doing qualitative research: Research methods for primary care* (Vol. 3). Newbury Park, CA: Sage.

Creegan, C. L. (1989). *Wittgenstein and Kierkegaard: Religion, individuality, and philosophical method.* London: Routledge.

Creswell, J. W. (1994). *Research design: Qualitative and quantitative approaches.* Thousand Oaks, CA: Sage.

Cutter, H. S. G., Boyatzis, R. E., & Clancy, D. D. (1977). Effectiveness of power motivation training in rehabilitating alcoholics. *Journal of Studies on Alcohol, 38,* 131-141.

Dailey, C. A. (1971). *Assessment of lives: Personality evaluation in a bureaucratic society.* San Francisco: Jossey-Bass.

Denzin, N. K., & Lincoln, Y. S. (Eds.). (1994). *Handbook of qualitative research.* Thousand Oaks, CA: Sage.

Diesing, P. (1971). *Patterns of discovery in the social sciences.* New York: Aldine.

Dreyfus, C. (1990). *The characteristics of high performing managers of scientists and engineers.* Unpublished doctoral dissertation, Case Western Reserve University.

Durrell, L. (1961). *Balthazar.* New York: Pocket.

Feshbach, S., & Singer, R. D. (1971). *Television and aggression: An experimental field study.* San Francisco: Jossey-Bass.

Flanagan, J. C. (1954). The critical incident technique. *Psychological Bulletin, 51,* 327-335.

Freud, A. (1966). *The writings of Anna Freud: Vol. 2. The ego and the mechanisms of defense.* New York: International Universities Press. (Original work published 1936)

Freud, S. (1965). *The interpretation of dreams.* New York: Avon. (Original work published 1900)

Fromm, E. (1951). *The forgotten language: An introduction to the understanding of dreams, fairy tales and myths.* New York: Grove.

Gottschalk, L. A. (1995). *Content analysis of verbal behavior: New findings and clinical applications.* Hillsdale, NJ: Lawrence Erlbaum.

Hill, B. (1967). *Gates of horn and ivory: An anthology of dreams.* New York: Taplinger.

Hobson, J. A. (1988). *The dreaming brain: How the brain creates both the sense and the nonsense of dreams.* New York: Basic Books.

Holsti, O. R. (1968). Content analysis. In G. Lindsey & E. Aronson (Eds.), *Handbook of social psychology* (2nd ed., Vol. 2, pp. 596-692). Reading, MA: Addison-Wesley.

How deputy stresses brains over brawn in battling gangs. (1988, December 29). *Wall Street Journal,* p. A8.

Howard, A., & Bray, D. (1988). *Managerial lives in transition: Advancing age and changing times.* New York: Guilford.

Jick, T. D. (1979). Mixing qualitative and quantitative methods: Triangulation in action. *Administrative Science Quarterly, 24,* 602-611.

Jung, C. G. (1961). *Memories, dreams, reflections.* New York: Vintage.

Jung, C. G. (1964). *Man and his symbols.* New York: Dell.

Kirk, J., & Miller, M. L. (1986). *Reliability and validity in qualitative research.* Beverly Hills, CA: Sage.

Klinger, E. (1971). *Structure and functions of fantasy.* New York: John Wiley.

Kolb, D. A. (1984). *Experiential learning: Experience as the source of learning and development.* Englewood Cliffs, NJ: Prentice Hall.

Kotter, J. P. (1982). *The general managers.* New York: Free Press.

Lee, R. B. (1979). *The Dobe !Kung.* New York: Holt, Rinehart & Winston.

Leonard, D., Fambrough, M., & Rhee, K. (1995). *A competency model of project managers.* Unpublished report to the National Aeronautics and Space Administration, Lewis Center, Cleveland.

Li, H., Rosenthal, R., & Rubin, D. B. (1996). Reliability of measurement in psychology: From Spearman-Brown to maximal reliability. *Psychological Methods, 1,* 98-107.

Loevinger, J., Wessler, R., & Redmore, C. (1983). *Measuring ego development: Vol. 2. Scoring manual for women and girls.* San Francisco: Jossey-Bass.

Luthans, F., Hodgetts, R. M., & Rosenkranz, S. A. (1988). *Real managers.* New York: Ballinger.

Marshall, C., & Rossman, G. (1989). *Designing qualitative research.* Newbury Park, CA: Sage.

Mason, J. (1996). *Qualitative researching.* Thousand Oaks, CA: Sage.

McAdams, D. P. (1985). *Power, intimacy and the life story: Personological inquiries into identity.* Homewood, IL: Dorsey.

McClelland, D. C. (1961). *The achieving society.* Princeton, NJ: D. Van Nostrand.

McClelland, D. C. (1973). Testing for competence rather than intelligence. *American Psychologist, 28,* 1-40.

McClelland, D. C. (1974). *How and why to code historical documents as the psychological interpretation of history.* Unpublished manuscript. Cambridge, MA: Harvard.

McClelland, D. C. (1985). *Human motivation.* Glenview, IL: Scott, Foresman.

McClelland, D. C. (in press). *Assessing competencies: Use of behavioral interviews to assess competencies associated with executive success.* Boston: McBer.

McClelland, D. C., Davis, W. N., Kalin, R., & Wanner, E. (1972). *The drinking man: Alcohol and human motivation.* New York: Free Press.

Mentkowski, M., McEachern, W., O'Brien, K., & Fowler, D. (1982). *Developing a professional competence model for management education.* Unpublished final report to the National Institutes of Education from Alverno College, Milwaukee.

Miles, M. B., & Huberman, A. M. (1984). *Qualitative data analysis: A sourcebook of new methods.* Beverly Hills, CA: Sage.

Miller, G. A. (1956). The magical number seven, plus or minus two: Some limits on our capacity for processing information. *Psychological Review, 63,* 81-97.

Miller, W., & Crabtree, B. F. (1992). Primary care research: A multimethod typology and qualitative road map. In B. F. Crabtree & W. L. Miller (Eds.), *Doing qualitative research: Research methods for primary care* (Vol. 3). Newbury Park, CA: Sage.

Moss, C. S. (1967). *The hypnotic investigation of dreams.* New York: John Wiley.

Motowidlo, S. J., Carter, G. W., Dunnette, M. D., Tippins, N., Werner, S., Burnett, J. R., & Vaughan, M. J. (1992). Studies of the structured behavioral interview. *Journal of Applied Psychology, 77,* 571-587.

Murray, H. A. (1959). *Myth and mythmaking.* Boston: Beacon.

Patton, M. Q. (1990). *Qualitative evaluation and research methods* (2nd ed.). Newbury Park, CA: Sage.

Rosenthal, R., & Rosnow, R. L. (1969). The volunteer subject. In R. Rosenthal & R. L. Rosnow (Eds.), *Artifact in behavioral research.* New York: Academic Press.

Rowland, W. D., Jr., & Watkins, B. (Eds.). (1984). *Interpreting television: Current research perspectives.* Beverly Hills, CA: Sage.

Schroder, H. M. (1989). *Managerial competence: The key to excellence.* Dubuque, IA: Kendall/Hunt.

Silverman, D. (1993). *Interpreting qualitative data: Methods for analyzing talk, text, and interaction.* Thousand Oaks, CA: Sage.

Smith, C. P. (1992). Reliability issues. In C. P. Smith, J. W. Atkinson, D. C. McClelland, & J. Veroff (Eds.), *Motivation and personality: Handbook of thematic content analysis.* New York: Cambridge University Press.

Smith, C. P., Feld, S. C., & Franz, C. E. (1992). Methodological considerations: Steps in research employing content analysis systems. In C. P. Smith, J. W. Atkinson, D. C. McClelland, & J. Veroff (Eds.), *Motivation and personality: Handbook of thematic content analysis.* New York: Cambridge University Press.

Spencer, L. M., Jr. (1995, November). *The economic value of competencies: Measuring the ROI of your training and development programs.* Paper presented at the Second International Conference of Using Competency-Based Tools and Applications to Drive Organizational Performance, Boston.

Spencer, L. M., Jr., & Spencer, S. M. (1993). *Competence at work: Models for superior performance.* New York: John Wiley.

Stamping out TV violence: A losing fight. (1993, October 26). *Wall Street Journal,* p. B1.

Stevens, A. (1995). *Private myths: Dreams and dreaming.* Cambridge, MA: Harvard University Press.

Stone, P.J., Dunphy, D. C., Smith, M. S., & Ogilvie, D. M. (1966). *The general inquirer: A computer approach to content analysis.* Cambridge, MA: MIT Press.

Strauss, A., & Corbin, J. (1990). *Basics of qualitative research: Grounded theory procedures and techniques.* Newbury Park, CA: Sage.

Thorton, G. C., III, & Byham, W. C. (1982). *Assessment centers and managerial performance.* New York: Academic Press.

Valliant, G. E. (1992). *Ego mechanisms of defense: A guide for clinicians and researchers.* Washington, DC: American Psychiatric Press.

Weitzman, E. A., & Miles, M. B. (1995). *A software sourcebook: Computer programs for qualitative data analysis.* Thousand Oaks, CA: Sage.

Winter, D. G. (1973). *The power motive.* New York: Free Press.

Winter, D. G. (1979). *An introduction to LMET theory and research: Task planning document EG-29B on Contract N00600-78-D-0564.* Boston: McBer.

Winter, D. G. (1992). Content analysis of archival materials, personal documents, and everyday verbal productions. In C. P. Smith, J. W. Atkinson, D. C. McClelland, & J. Veroff (Eds.), *Motivation and personality: Handbook of thematic content analysis.* New York: Cambridge University Press.

Winter, D. G., & Healy, J. M., Jr. (1981, August). *An integrated system for scoring motives in running text: Reliability, validity, and convergence.* Paper presented at the annual meeting of the American Psychological Association, Los Angeles.

Winter, D. G., & McClelland, D. C. (1978). Thematic analysis: An empirically derived measure of the effects of liberal arts education. *Journal of Educational Psychology, 70,* 8-16.

Winter, D. G., & Stewart, A. J. (1977). Power motive reliability as afunction of retest instructions. *Journal of Consulting and Clinical Psychology, 45,* 436-440.

Wolcott, H. F. (1994). *Transforming qualitative data: Description analysis, and interpretation.* Thousand Oaks, CA: Sage.

Zyzanski, S. J., McWhinney, I. R., Blake, R. B., Jr., Crabtree, B. F., & Miller, W. L. (1992). Qualitative research: Perspectives on the future. In B. F. Crabtree & W. L. Miller (Eds.), *Doing qualitative research: Research methods for primary care* (Vol. 3). Newbury Park, CA: Sage.

Index

About the Author

Richard E. Boyatzis is Professor of Organizational Behavior, Chair of the Department of Organizational Behavior, and Associate Dean for Executive Education Programs at the Weatherhead School of Management at Case Western Reserve University (CWRU), Cleveland. His main areas of research are adult development and leadership. Before joining the faculty at CWRU, he was President and CEO of McBer & Co. from 1976 to 1987 and had been with McBer since 1969. From 1983 to 1985, he was an executive with Yankelovich, Skelly & White, while on its Board of Directors and the Board of the Reliance Consulting Group. From 1985 to 1986, he was on the Board of the Hay Group when they were owned by Saatchi & Saatchi. He has consulted to many Fortune 500 companies, government agencies, and companies in Europe on various topics, including executive and management development, organization structure, culture change, R&D productivity, economic development, selection, promotion, performance appraisal, and career pathing. He is the author of numerous articles on human motivation, self-directed behavior change, leadership, value trends, managerial competencies, power, and alcohol and aggression, and he is the author of a research book entitled *The Competent Manager: A Model for Effective Performance* (1982). He is also a coauthor of *Innovations in Professional Education: Steps on a*

Journey From Teaching to Learning with Scott S. Cowen and David A. Kolb. He has a BS in aeronautics and astronautics from MIT and an MA and PhD in social psychology from Harvard University.